OUR UNIVERSE

OUR UNIVERSE

TRANSLATED FROM THE ORIGINAL BENGALI
OF RABINDRANATH TAGORE BY

INDU DUTT

Foreword by
MALCOLM MACDONALD

JAICO PUBLISHING HOUSE
MUMBAI ● DELHI ● CALCUTTA
BANGALORE ● HYDERABAD ● CHENNAI

OUR UNIVERSE
ISBN 81-7224-727-3

First Jaico Impression : 1999
Second Jaico Impression : 2000

Published by:
Ashwin J. Shah
Jaico Publishing House
121, M.G. Road,
Mumbai-400 023

Printed by:
Gayatri Offset Press
A-66, Sector-2, Noida-201301

CONTENTS

DEDICATION

"This translation is dedicated
to the memory of the author
whose works have offered
the greatest eduction in my life."

Malcolm MacDonald in his foreword to this, the second volume of Indu Dutt's translations, says of the Bengali poet: Rabindranath Tagore was a man whose interests were as varied as his output was prolific. He was poet, dramatist, essayist and novelistl; he composed his own music for his own countless songs; he had considerable independent influence in the politics of his day; he was an educationist who founded the famous school and university of Santiniketan; he was thinker and teacher and reformer; and he was much else besides.

Amongst other things he felt a deep interest in scientific speculation and discovery. For him the planet Earth was only a small, though marvellously significant speck in Creation, and he believed that if we are to understand ourselves we must comprehend also the Universe of which our world is a mere particle. One of his finest abilities was his capacity for interpreting Nature, and his love of Nature, which in one aspect was localized enthusiastically in the landscapes of Bengal, extended infinitely to the stars hormoniously crowding space. His appetite to learn about them was unlimited and this book reveals how exact and wide was his grasp of contemporary knowledge on the subject. It is a book by a student for fellow-students; but it is also a poet's description of what he gleaned from countless learned scientific works, and has a simplicity combined with imagery that makes his account very vivid.

Indu Dutt's own discriminating taste for words, and her devotion to Rabindranath's spirit, have enabled her to give a distinguished interpretation of his work.

FOREWORD

by Malcolm MacDonald

I remember, when I was a child, being enthralled one day by the appearance of a stranger sitting, talking with my father in his library. At first I thought that he was one of the prophets stepped from the Old Testament. His hair was shoulder-length, his beard was long and fine, and his handsome figure was dressed in flowing robes which touched the floor. But what struck me most—and has remained in my memory ever since—was his face. It had a Christ-like nobility, gentleness, sadness and lovingness.

I learnt his name when my father introduced me to him.

"This is Rabindranath Tagore," I heard.

To my unaccustomed, infant Western ears it sounded like a strange poem with an echo of music.

Rabindranath Tagore was a tremendous figure not only in the Indian literature but also in the national life of his times. In a generation of many memorable and some immortal Indians, when Indian history was being made on a grand scale, he stood pre-eminent with only two or three others as a spokesman of his countrymen's character, aspirations and will.

But he was more than a great Indian. There is no doubt of the truth of Edward Thomspon's judgment on Rabindranath, that "the assessment of final values cannot be done in this generation; but already it is clear that his ultimate place will be not simply among India's poets, but among those of the world".

Yet the world is so far scarcely aware of this. One reason is that comparatively few of his works have been translated into English, which is not only the language of the Anglo-Saxon peoples but also now a chief means of communication and understanding between the various races of mankind. It is important that English volumes of his writing should be multiplied, so that different nations round the Earth may be uplifted by his beauty of expression, his breadth of wisdom and his loftiness of spirit. But the translations will be inadequate unless they render faithfully his own richness of words.

Mrs Indu Dutt has already published one slim volume of translation called **A Tagore Testament.** It included some of Rabindrananth's autobiographical essays and poems which illumine two profound qualities in him: his boundless joy in life, and his passionate awareness of an unseen and unknown force in his being, guiding his work, whom he describes as "He who sits behind my eyes". Mrs Dutt's translations abundantly deserved the praise which they received. Now she launches another venture, translation of his book **Bishwa-Parichaya,** called **Our Universe**.

Tagore was a man whose interests were as varied as his output was prolific. He was poet, dramatist, essayist and novelist; he composed his own music for his own countless songs; he had considerable independent influence in the politics of his day; he was an educationist who founded the famous school and university at Shantiniketan; he was thinker and teacher and reformer and he was much else besides.

Amongst other things he felt a deep interest in scientific speculation and discovery. For him the planet Earth was only a small, though marvellously significant speck in Creation, and he believed that if we are to understand ourselves we must comprehend also the Universe of which our world is a mere particle. One of his finest abilities was his capacity for interpreting Nature, and his love of Nature, which in one aspect was localized enthusiastically in the landscape of Bengal, extended infinitely to the stars harmoniously crowding space. His appetite to learn about them was unlimited, and this book reveals how exact and wide was his grasp of contemporary knowledge on the subject. It is a book by a student for fellow students; but it is also a poet's description of what he gleaned from countless learned scientific works, and has a simplicity combined with imagery that makes his account very vivid. But though he marvelled at every fresh discovery of the scientists, beyond each little new addition to knowledge Creation remained for him a source of deep wonder, unyielding of explanation, transcending human reckoning.

Indu Dutt's own discriminating taste for words, and her devotion to Rabindrananth's spirit, have enabled her to give a distinguished interpretation of his work. I am no authority on Tagore, nor on the Indian literature of which he is such a shining light, nor on the Universe which so fascinated him, nor indeed on any other aspect of his interests. I am just one of the innumerable non-Indians who is eager to know more about him. Like them, I am grateful to Indu Dutt for what she is doing to introduce him to us, I admire that skill with which she does it, and I hope that she will persevere in the great service which she is performing for the memory of the great master and for the enlightenment of his world-wide audience.

Whoever wishes,
May he sit in meditation
With eyes closed
To verify if the universe be
true or false.
I, in the meanwhile,
Shall sit with insatiate eyes
To see the universe
While the light lasts.

To

Sreejut Satyendra Nath Basu

I have linked your name with this book. I am aware that it holds no such scientific treatise that I can place it in your hands without some hesitation. Moreover, for fear that I may be a trespasser, I do not feel quite at ease... perhaps this is no proper way of showing respect to you! Having had a few authentic books before me I had to adopt drastic weeding measures. And there is much that has been weeded. Nevertheless, after my daring example if some man of genius with a taste for literature and who is a scientist as well, takes upon himself this work as a necessary and important duty, I shall know my attempt has had its recompense.

It is urgent that those who have begun their education should be allowed from the very start to enter the outer gate of science if not quite into its threshold. It is here that literature can help to pave the way for science, and for this, science need feel no compunction. It is with this sense of responsibility that I have undertaken this work, though I am aware I am answerable not only to literature but to science as well. The slightest departure from the accuracy of truth, or a slip in the correctness of expression science never forgives. Within my limited range I have been careful about these. In fact, though a sense of duty has guided me to write, it is not so much out of a sense of duty towards any pupil as towards myself. As I wrote I had to teach myself continually. Perhaps this conditioning of a student's mind in me will find a beneficent response in the aspiring minds of some students.

I am afraid I shall have to elaborate my apologies so that you may understand clearly the psychology of mind that made me write.

The vast universe hides itself in the very minute, dwarfs itself in the vast enormity, or obliterates itself, moving away behind the scenes. It presents itself before us with all the features of its appearance arranged in a way that is held within the framework of man's natural intelligence. But man, whatever else he may be, is not natural. He is the only being who questioned his natural sense, challenged it, and has been glad when he had defeated it. To reach a shore beyond this natural sense, man has brought the distant near, made the unseen visible, and has found words for the inexplicable. In the world of the unmanifest within the heart of the manifest—in this dense depth—man has made his entry constantly trying to unravel the mystery that lies at the root of all the happenings in the universe. The will to make this a success, the opportunity and strength that are needed, can be claimed by very few people on this earth. Those who are deprived of the blessings of such gifts and the aim of purpose, live in utter segregation from all related activities of the modern age.

In a large forest the trees shed their dry leaves one by one in profusion thus making the soil underneath fertile. In a country where there is continuous research in science, becoming fertile with an alive feeling in science, knowledge of it in fragmentary bits is being spread constantly. This is how one's heart's soil is quickened, becoming fertile with an alive feeling in science. It is the loss of it that has left our mind unscientific. We feel the impoverishment not only in our education, but also in the field of our occupation where we are bowed with frustration.

When the non-experts like us make an effort to remove some difficulties; it is bound to cause great amusement, especially amongst those who are also non-experts like us. On my behalf there is something that I will say. A mother feels an anxiety for her child, though she may not have the knowledge of a doctor. The knowledge can be borrowed, but not the feeling of concern. In nursing, this feeling of concern has a positive savour that is not to be ignored.

Needless to say I am no devotee of science, but since childhood I have always been curious about it, deriving endless pleasure from it. I remember when I was about nine or ten years old, often on a Sunday, Sreejut Sita Nath Datta would pay us a visit. His stock of knowledge was not great, this I know today. But at the time when by demonstrating he would explain some very rudimentary truths about science to me, my eyes widened. I remember he showed me once how when being heated the water at the bottom of a container would become lighter and rise to the surface, while the heavier water on the top would sink. Moreover, he would emphasize the fact by mixing a few grains of saw-dust in, and I was so astonished at the thought that there should be such a difference in density between two layers of the same water at the same time, that I can still recall my reaction to it. I came to realize then for the fist time that a happening that I once took as a natural sequence without giving it a second thought, was not after all so simple a matter. Later when I was about twelve (I must warn you that I am rather date-blind as some people are about colour), my father and I visited the hill station Dalhousie. After whole day's meandering we used to return to our rest house in the evening, when my father sat back in his chair in the open courtyard. There, straight before us, the dense blue sky appeared with its hedge of mountain ranges, and in the clear darkness the stars descended close to us. My father used to point out the stars, the planets to me. More than that, he related to me in detail the distances of their orbits from the sun, the time they took in their revolution and so on. All that he said I could remember so clearly that I even wrote a lengthy essay in my still immature style. I wrote because I felt joy in it. This was my first essay that came out in serial form, and it happened to be on a scientific theme.

Some years passed. I found by then that I could use the English language quite intelligently and guess correctly. I would get hold of any scientific books on astronomy that I found easy to read. Sometimes the intricacies of mathematics would lead me on to rugged ground, but I would mercilessly drag myself over it. From this I have learnt one lesson, that in life in the first flush of our experience it is not always that we understand everything, nor can we say that because of this we lag behind in our journey. Like land and water there is a partition in our understanding, so that more than what we see there is a lot that we do not see, and yet we survive and, what is more, we experience joy. To a certain extent not understanding can even be an incentive to our progress. I never forgot this when teaching my students. In class many a time I have presented the text-books of the older students to my younger students. I cannot in the least account for all that they learnt, but there are things outside all customary calculations which if they did learn could do them no harm. This particular understanding claims no right where the examiner's pencil marks are involved, but has its own special virtue. At least in my life I can say that much of me would be left out if I had to deduct when I gained by such reading.

I started to read simpler books on astronomy. Many books on the subject were already published. The huge volume of Sir Robert Ball gave me great satisfaction. To follow it up, and much enthused, I read other authors like Newcombe and Flamryon—devouring them all from beginning to end. Then at one time I also ventured upon a set of articles on physiology by Huxley. Astronomy and physiology were the two subjects that had always engrossed my attention. This, I admit, was no profound learning, for it lacked the strength of a scholarly foundation. But being in constant touch through reading I naturally developed a disposition to science. My disregard for all blind and absurd superstitions has saved me I hope, from allowing my ideas to become diffused. And yet, at the same time I do feel that this has never been hindrance to me in the field of poetry or in the realm of imagination.

Today at the conclusion of my life-chapter I remain overwhelmed with the newest phase in natural science—in the magic of scientific theories. All that I read before, I could not wholly understand. But I continued to read. Today it seems the same. Much of what I read is still beyond my understanding. What is more, it is even beyond some of the scholarly pundits.

Those who find food for their mind from the source of science, are devotees. 'The sweetmeats are for the common mind'—this enjoyment I do claim. This is not a thing to be proud of, but if the mind is glad, that is its own reward. This is the result of that reward. I have systematically gone from door to door filling my alms-bowl to gather its material.

Not being scholarly, it is obvious that there is no scholarly stress in this book. My concern has been for the appropriate language. There is a need for technical terms in proper scientific training. But technical terms, like food, are to be chewed. They can only be prescribed when the teeth are ready for them. With this in my mind I have avoided technical terms, preferring the simple style.

You will notice one thing in the book—in the medium or, in other words, in the language which I have used I have tried consciously to make it simple for general understanding, though I have not deemed it right to lighten its contents by reducing its weight superficially. To deprive anyone of anything through pity is not kindness. It is my conviction that people, however immature, will absorb as much as they can within their capacity. If they fail they will give up their struggle, but it would be lacking in consideration if they were served with a mearge meal. A subject that needs to be studied and is not purely a matter for entertainment cannot be fathomed by merely glancing through it. Application and an active effort to understand are both a part of learning, they go hand in hand with the joy one has. This the experience I gethered myself from being almost self-educated from my childhood. At one age I hated milk, and I would play up to my elders by steadily stirring and raising it to a frothy height up to the drink of my bowl. I have seen authors who in writing children's books, show a similar trick by introducing frothy, foamy stuff. They forget that if there is joy in knowledge, it also has its price. If in childhood one gets into the habit of escaping this price, one escapes the possession of joy. It is by chewing one's food that one's teeth are strengthened, deriving at the same time the full flavour of the food. I had this in view when writing this book.

Sreejut Pramatha Nath Sen Gupta. M.Sc., was your former

student. He is now lecturer in science at the Santiniketan Institute. In the beginning I had handed over to him the responsibility of this book, but gradually, by degrees, it came to rest on me. Had he not, however, begun the book I could never have finished it. Besides, my own unbusiness-like method would have lost all courage on this untrodden road. I have received from him encouragement, as well as active help.

In the quiet surroundings of Almorah I was able to complete this work. I was also very fortunate in having my dear friend Boshi Sen with me. He went through the whole manuscript carefully, and enjoyed it, which is my greatest reward.

During my illness my colleague Sreejut Rajshekar Basu made some corrections in the proof, thus helping me considerably towards its publication. I am grateful to him.

Rabindranath Tagore.

Santiniketan,
2nd, Ashvin 1344. (September. 1937)

1

The emerald became green in the hue of my consciousness,
The ruby became red.
I opened my eyes to the skies,
And light broke from East to West.
I looked at the rose and said, 'How beautiful!'
And the rose became beautiful.
You will say, 'These are philosophical truths,
These are not the poet's speech.'
I say, 'These are truths,
And what is poetry but truth?'

My conceit is here,
A conceit on behalf of mankind;
On the canvas of man's conceit is drawn
the masterpiece of universe—
The creation of the Artist.

The philosopher reiterates at every breath
Counting his rosary,
"There is no emerald, no ruby, no light and no rose,
Neither you nor me',
While He who is infinite came to realise Himself
Within the boundary of man,
And this is named 'I'.

In the density of that 'I' a conflict arose
Between shadow and light.
There appeared form, the awakening of sap.
The 'no' became 'yes' at an unknown moment
In line, colour, grief and joy.
Do not tell me these are philosophical truths!
My heart fills with delight
As I stand with brush in hand and paint,
In the creative ground of the universal 'I'.

The Pandit has said...
That old moon,
It has a cruel cunning smile.
It is creeping nearer and nearer to the heart of the earth
With the message of Death.
A day will come when it will strike
A final blow to her rocks and seas.
In Eternity's new recording book,
There will be a cipher covering the page of this planet.
It will blot out the totality of her days and nights.

Man's deeds will lose all pretence of immortality,
Man's history will merge into the ink of eternal night,
Man in his farewell glance will take away the colour of the
    universe,
Man's mind on that final day will leave no trace
Of a fulfilling seed.
The tremor of power will rage from sky to sky,

No light will shine.
In the great concert-hall without a lute,
The performer's fingers will move in the rhythm of a dance
But with no music.

That day God, losing all poetry, will reman alone
Seated under a blue-less sky,
Bent on a mathematical calculation devoid of personal element,
When in this vast universe
No voice will rise amongst countless people,
From life to life, far or near,
To echo, 'I love you', 'You are beautiful'.

Will then God once again sit in ageless contemplation,
And repeat His prayers from amid night's devastation,
Saying 'Speak, oh speak!'
Uttering, 'Say, you are beautiful',
'Say, I am in love?'

THE WORLD OF ATOMS

When we are born, our body is alive with certain inherent faculties, such as the faculty to see, to hear, to smell, to taste and to touch. These are called senses. Our likes and dislikes, happiness and sorrow are all mingled with our senses.

All our perception is limited to a degree. After all, how far can we possibly see, to what extent are we able to hear? Similarly, the other remaining senses also have their own limitations. This really means that whatever resources we have through our faculties are for the sole purpose of our struggle for survival. Beyond that we may have a little extra in our hands, and this is what makes us reach the human sphere, stepping out of the animal world.

The planet out of which the earth is born, and by whose rays it is nourished, is the sun. All around us the sun hangs up its curtains of light. They do not allow us to see what exists in the universe outside the earth. But when the day ends, the sun sets, and the covering light is removed, millions of stars appear against the darkness. We know then that the universe expands far beyond the boundary of this earth. But how far it extends we cannot truly conceive with our senses.

The only link that we have with this distance is through our eyes. No sound comes from there as it is through air that the sound perception arises. Air envelopes the earth like a shroud. It is air that causes sound on the earth. Along with our touch sensation we have yet another feeling, the feeling that we are hot or cold. The feelings has its origin outside the earth. The sun emits rays, we get warmth from the rays. In this warmth is our life. There are planets which are a million times larger than the sun. Their rays do not touch our senses. But the sun is no stranger to us. Of all the heavenly bodies that make up the vast universe, the sun is the only planet intimately related to us, though there is the fact that the sun is not near to us. The distance is considerable, it is nearly 93,000,000 miles. This may sound startling, and yet this is the smallest distance from the world of planets to the world we live in, and the lowest in the range of all our calculations. There are no other planets or stars nearer to the earth.

When we imagine these vast distances we are filled with awe, because our world, this global earth made of water and soil, is comparatively very small. When we walk round the earth, its longest line, the line encircling the equator, is only about 25,000 miles long. The more we advance in the knowledge of the universe, the more we realize that in the history of size and distance 25,000 miles measure little. Our perception, as it has been already pointed out, has a very limited range. Our everyday experience of distances is not great. What we do and what we see are circumscribed within our allotted distances.

But as the curtain is raised, the universe in its diminutive form appears within the narrow range of our perception, and gives us a hint of its larger presence otherwise we would have never known it! For our eyes are not fitted for seeing all. The animals accept the limitations of their eyes. They are satisfied with whatever may come within the grasp of their natural powers. But it is different with man. The organs of his perception merely act as indicators. But more than his sense perception is the extent of his intellect. It has the audacity to run a challenging race with almost anything in the world. It has busied itself in exploring the vast measurements of this immense universe, nullifying all the childish reports of the unrealistic mind. We cannot fully fathom a distance of 93,000,000 miles with our senses. But intellect refused to own defeat, it occupied itself with mathematical calculation.

Apart from the extensive world around us, even when we come to consider the world we live in—which could in no way be nearer—we still fail to realize it fully with any of our senses. But if we see a map of it drawn on a small globe, we get some idea of its fundamental form. In size the world is many thousand times larger than the globe. This introductory sketch on the globe is only drawn by our perception of sight without any other senses participating in it. From the point of view of full detail, it holds no solid proof. Because our power of seeing is limited, we see things only in their dwarfed state.

Similarly, as the universe appears each night revealing itself above us on the globe of the sky we accept it in its much smaller version. No other senses are responsible for it except our power of observation. What is beyond our imagination, comes within our grasp when seen in the outlined enclosure of the sky.

To have an idea that how minimized this size has been, we have to hold it against the sun for comparison. Naturally we consider our world as the largest of all that we know or can visualize. We are able to see it though in its parts. With our senses we could never absorb the whole of it at the same time. The sun is yet 1,300,000 million times bigger than the earth. Vast though as it is, it appears no bigger than a round golden tray in a corner of the sky. When we are told of the vast tumultuous activities that take place in the sun, and then at dawn each day we see the sun rising slowly like a golden disc from behind our mango-grove, delighting the heart of all, man or beast, every shrub and tree, we realize the delusion that we live in! We are being assured that in our everyday survival we have no need to know more. It is just as well, for otherwise how could we have lived at all! For, if the sun with all the splendour of its presence came within the slightest reach of our senses we would perish long ago. This applies as far as the sun is concerned. There are myriads of stars which are even bigger than the sun. They appear to us like specks of light. The distances that these stars cover are beyond our comprehension. This vastness of the sky as the dwelling place of the universe we may try to estimate from another angle. A great message with its great force comes form the outside of our world and this gives us the sensation of heat. This is but the warmth of the sun. The message comes from a distance of 93,000,000 miles. Moreover, the same sky holds millions and millions of other stars; in some of them the heat is even more intense than the sun's. But fortunately for us their accumulated heat perishes on its way to us, so that in this conflagration of the universe the sky remains still bearable to us—so distant is this path, and so immense the sky! Compared to these a distance of 93,000,000 miles through which the heat has to travel before it touches our sensation is small. To sit by a kitchen fire that is being prepared for a colossal feast is by no means comforting. Yet, to live in a town at midday when every household has its kitchen fire lighted, is possible, because the heat is spread out in the much larger sky. What happens in the world of stars is actually the same. There, however vast the preparations of fire may be, the encompassing sky is infinitely larger.

What is it then that brings us the news of these stars' existence from such an unfathomable distance? The simple answer is light. But light is not just a static matter that sits muttering the news to us. It is like a messenger, swift on its errand, runs as it carries its news on its back—this is the greatest discovery of science. It does not run at an ordinary pace, it has a speed that is unrivalled by any other couriers in the universe. We are the people of a small world, that is why the knowledge of a speed that is the fastest in the universe has so long escaped us, till one day the scientist discovered the miraculous fact that light travels 186,000 miles a second. Such a speed is worked out by mathematicians. We could hardly conceive it otherwise. Our intellect proves where our perception fails. To know the nature of the speed of light with our senses, we need to be on a bigger space than the earth. Within this restricted space its speed has appeared to us almost static. Its proof can only be found in the great outer space. The sun remaining in this outer space is at a great distance from us—a distance notwithstanding how many millions of miles it may be, that is nevertheless very small according to the measurements of the Zodiacal world.

It follows then that within this comparatively small distance man found it possible to witness the speed of light. He got the message that the light from the sun crossed the void, reaching the earth in about eight and a half minutes. In other words, when the sun actually comes within the range of our sight, it has already appeared before then. It takes about eight and a half minutes for the courier light to make the announcement of its arrival. This delay is not of much consequence, for the news we receive is fresh. But in the case of the nearest star in the solar system, which amongst all the planets we may call our neighbour, when it lets us know of its existence, the light takes four years to bring the message to us. This means that at the moment we receive the news it is already four years old. We could draw the line here. Nevertheless we are also told there are stars even more remote, whose light reaches us after several millions of years.

In discovering this movement of light in the sky science was confronted with another question, 'What is then the nature of this movement?' The fact was also a miraculous one. The answer was found that light's movements are like subtle waves. But what were these waves nobody was able to tell. All that could be found out from light's behaviour was that it moved like waves. But man's mind was defeated when simultaneously an equally important message came forward with all its convincing proofs to tell us that light was composed of myriads of meteoric small particles, continuously pouring down like very minute sparkling fragments. How exactly these two contradictory reports intermingle we do not know. What is more extraordinary is the nature of the two opposing facts. What we see from the outside as waves and the force of a shower but within which we find neither one nor the other, we call light—how this is possible the pundits have failed to explain.

A question that may easily crop up in our mind is how then such a tremendous and subtle fact could ever be discovered, a fact that the mind cannot register, that is beyond our seeing or hearing. Yet there are proofs, proofs that are positive and which we can only accept. People who have collected such evidence have gone through extreme hardship to gain knowledge, they have travelled formidable paths with their inquiries. Very few of us possess the knowledge or the intelligence that is required to verify their statements. Ignorant as we are if we disbelieve them we will be deceiving ourselves. The path to evidence is always open. If we aspire and continue to follow this path, if we earn the merit, we shall one day, no doubt, have answers to all our questions.

For the time being let us see what this wave of light means. This light-wave is not a continuous flow of a preceding wave. Many other waves have joined it in a group. Some are visible, and some are not. It is better to point out here that light which we do not see has not the same name in our everyday vocabulary. But visible or invisible, when both have a tendency to raise a similar kind of waves of a certain energy they do not deserve in the encyclopedia of the universe to have different names. It is like two brothers when one is well known and the other is not, yet both are entitled to bear the same surname according to the family order.

There is yet another wave that comes under the same group of these light-waves. We cannot see it, we only feel it by touch. This is the heat-wave. It has the greatest power for production. Amongst all the substances in the nature of a light-wave, some we see, some we know by touch, some we distinctly see as light and feel their warmth simultaneously; but some are never seen, some are beyond our touch. If we have to attribute a common name to this crowded group of light-waves, whether revealed or unrevealed, we may describe it as energy. In the beginning of or after or throughout the creation of the universe there is the vibration of this energy in different states of being either evident or concealed. Even in a stone or in iron there is a movement within, which when we look at it from outside we are not aware of. It seems the embodiment of stillness. And yet it has been proved that all the fine substance like atoms and molecules that constitute its whole structure, and which are not visible to our eyes, are in a constant state of vibration. When it is cold it also vibrates, and as the vibration increases it gets hotter and hotter until we can detect it with our senses. When heated in fire the molecules in iron begin to gather momentum till they become so violent that their agitation can no longer be suppressed. This wave of agitation strikes the sensation-chord in our body circulating a message which we call heat. In reality heat strikes us. Light beats upon our eyes, heat beats upon our body.

I remember when I was a child, our teacher once showed us how a piece of iron could at first be heated in the fire, it then became bright red, finally a dazzling white, and I worried myself to death to know what could possible be this property in fire which when applied externally could so entirely change the composition of iron. We are told today that when heated further iron becomes gas. These are the magic performances of heat, and these have been happening since creation.

The light of the sun is white. Seven different coloured rays are mixed to make up these white rays. It is like a seven-coloured tail; when folded it looks white but reveals its seven colours when spread out. In the olden days we used to have chandeliers. They have now been abolished from our country since the discovery of electricity. These hanging chandeliers were composed of three-cornered glass prisms which had one virtue that when sunlight poured through them they broke it up, scattering its seven hues. The colours run in succession as violet, indigo, blue, green, yellow, orange and red. These seven rays become visible to the eye, but outside their two extremities there are other larger and smaller waves of similar energy that fail to come within the range of our normal perception. The wave of light that lies outside the violet ray is called ultra-violet ray. And the ray that fails to reach the red, lying outside its outer boundary, is called the infra-red ray. There we a great astronomer by the name of Sir William Horschell. He discovered through this three-cornered glass that light has seven coloured rays. With his darkened heat-measuring-equipment he started to test each ray. The heat became intenser as he went towards the red ray. When he took his instrument further beyond the red into the dark colourlessness, he found there was no lessening of heat. It became clear that there must be other rays that hid themselves in darkness. Then came another German physicist. He started his research work with a photographic plate. On his plate there were signs of the seven rays from the red to the violet. He then proceeded to search beyond the violet ray into the darkness. Here what eyes failed to see was registered on the plate which showed that the heat in the light was towards the red ray, its chemical activities leaned towards the violet. Once it was thought that the hidden rays were the close followers of the coloured rays, left behind in darkness. But as the research on these hidden rays became more and more advanced, the coloured rays began to take a humbler place. Today, in the estimation of science, light is not limited within its seven-rayed domain, its reigning range has expanded to a hundred times more. The wave that we found towards the infra-red light carries with it the message of the sky by which we get our radio news. The ray that was discovered on the side of the violet ray is the famous Roentgen ray. With its help we can see the deep-seated bones in our body through our covering skin.

Man has not only looked upon light as the conveyor of the stars' existence, he has also managed to find out the substance that mingle in its composition, tearing them as it were from the very heat of light. How this was arrived at has its explanation.

When sunlight passes through a three-sided glass we come face to face with its seven colours all in succession. If iron or some similar hard substance is heated to a point when it emits a white ray, we can see in its divided sections seven distinct colours side by side.There is no gap between them. But when with more heat the iron turns into gas, and its light breaks through the three-sided glass, the coloured streaks hold no continuous light. One sees separate, disjointed bright lines with gaps in between that are filled with no light. We may call this lay-out of sketch a spectrum.

From this chart we have seen that each substance when in a blazing gaseous state shows in its light different colour-streaks.

There is a basic element in salt that is known as sodium. When heated to a gaseous state we see in its colour-chart two adjacent yellow lines. No other colours are found. Substances that have no sodium in them do not show in their flames the same two coloured lines at the exact place. Whenever we see these two lines in the colour-chart of any gaseous object we know for certain that there is sodium.

But in the streaks of sunlight we find that these two bright yellow lines of sodium gas are stolen, being replaced by two black lines. The scientists tell us that when a light from any gaseous object passes through the same gaseous heat of a comparatively cooler nature, it becomes consumed. In which case it is not in the absence of light that these two black lines are being created. In reality, the amount of sodium gas that is seen in the colour-group of the sun impeding sunlight also scatters its own light as its heat will permit. This heat, being milder than the heat in the colour-orbit, shines less brightly. This fainter ray against the bright streaks of coloured light gives us the impression of its being black.

The colour-chart of every elemental substance has been already formed through this penetration into light. By analysing the differences in colour we come to detect different matters whatever they may be, provided they are in the same state of gaseous combustion.

The ninety-two elemental substances that have been found on the earth should also exist in the sun, because the earth's body is born of the sun. In the preliminary test only thirty-six elementary substances were found in the sun. What happened to the rest of the elements was a problem that was solved much later by Meghnad Saha, a Bengali scientist. He discovered a new path of investigation by which he found out a few more elements. Following his path nearly all the rest were recovered. A few are still untraced, being completely absorbed midway by the atmospheric air on earth.

All the colours in the sunlight blend, making it white. How

can we then see different colours in different things? The answer is that all things do not absorb all the colours, they exclude some, offering no reason. These rejected colours are our gain, a gift to our eyesight. The liquid that a thick blotting paper absorbs is of no use to us. The liquid that is surplus, that is left over is what we gain. It is exactly the same with sunlight. The ruby accepts from sunlight all its coloured waves but returns to it the red. In this renunciation lies the splendor of the ruby. Its glory is not in what it appropriates. What makes the ruby indifferent to the red, and the sapphire reject the blue is an answer that remains hidden in the innermost recess of their own molecules. White hair refuse all the colour-waves of the sunlight; that is why it is white. Black hair absorbs all its waves, or in other words it refuses to give up any section of the sunlight, that is why it is black. If all the objects in the world appropriated all the colours from the sun then our miserly world would appear as nothing but black; the colours would not show up at all! Like a postmaster who prevented all his postmen from delivering messages! On the other hand, if no colours were accepted, everything would appear white. All characteristics would be wiped out in that oneness of uniformity. It would be as though the messages that the postmen were to take to seven separate addresses were lumped into one, so that they lost their individual identity. When we see people as all alike, that is not seeing at all! We cannot see when things retain no light or absorb all light. We only see things in the fractions of light as they meet and assemble.

There are many other waves that are mixed with sun-light, and which come down in such small measure that we do not feel them. There are also other waves which come down in profusion, but the earth's atmospheric air resists them. Otherwise we would be set on fire and burnt to death. The sun's gift to us is as much as we can bear to receive, and with which all the machinery of our body has come to perfect terms from the beginning. All the ways and means we adopt for our everyday existence refuse to function outside this.

What mostly attracts our eye in the universal picture are the stars, and the sun which is but a star. All along they have taken prominence in man's mind. In this modern age what man has marvelled at is the world that is hidden within the visible world, a world that is subtle, which is not visible to the eye, and yet is at the root of all creation.

If we try to find out by examining a mud house what is its basic matter, we shall come across particles of dust. No matter how much we crush, there will be still a very fine grain of dust which we can describe as the first fundamental basis of a mud house. In the same manner man once thought that by dividing the matter of the universe, section by section, it would come to such a fine point that it would no longer be divisible, and this would be the primary material of the universe, or its basic element. In our Shastras it is known as 'Paramanu'. Scientist in Europe call it the atom. These atoms are so fine that if 10,000,000 of them are put side by side they will measure only about an inch.

A particle of dust cannot be further dissected by ordinary method. But science in its drive has been able to tackle all the materials of the universe reducing them to a much finer solution. It has ultimately ended with ninety-two pure elements. The pundits tell us that all that is in the universe is created out of these elements through the process of elimination and addition, the range of which is unending.

Let us suppose that one part of a mud hut is made of pure earth and the other is mixed with cow dung. If we break up its walls, we will find in the pounded mixture two separate ingredients, one of which is the pure grain of dust and the other the grain mixed with cow dung. In the same manner, the scientists, having tested all the material elements in the universe, have classified them into two groups. One is called the rudimentary, the other derivative. A rudimentary matter has no admixture, but a derivative matter is a mixture of one or more ingredients. Gold is rudimentary, for no matter how finely we may split it by natural process, it will still remain gold. Water is derivative, for when we divide water we come across two kinds of rudimentary gases in it. One is oxygen and the other hydrogen. When these two gases remain separate they retain their own individual virtue, but as soon as they are fused and become water, they are beyond recognition. A new behaviour arises from their union. All derivative matters meet with the same destiny. They hide within themselves all traces of their rudimentary element. At one time all substances worthy of the name of an atom earned the reputation of being the primal material of the universe. It was believed that they had reached the state when no further dissection was possible. But ultimately this material was also split. The substance we call an atom had still to go through a further breaking process, when an even subtler substance was found to exist in the heart of the atom. This was miracle substance. We even hesitate to call it a substance. This needs further explaining.

Today the word 'electricity' is very much in vogue—electric lights, electric torches, electric fans and many such things that are electric. Everybody is aware that electricity is but energy. We know that the lightning that flashes from amongst the clouds is also electricity. And it is this lightning that announces to the world the greatest power of electricity through flashes of light and peals of thunder. When it strikes our body, it is deadly.

Electricity is of two kinds. Scientist have named one as positive and the other as negative. When translated this means that one has 'the virtue', and the other 'no virtue'. They are opposing in nature. Everything that exists is at the mingling of these two opposites. And yet, there is a natural antipathy between one positive and another positive, or one negative and another negative. Their attraction is for the opposite.

We find that these two kinds of very subtle electric charge are grouped in the atom. The atom is bound in union with these two opposite charges as the sun is tied to the planets—in the solar system. As the sun in the centre of the solar system makes the earth revolve round it with its magnetic reins, the positive electric charge from the centre of the atom draw the negative ones towards them. And they in return like the circus horses in motion revolve round the positive ones which hold the reins in their hands.

The earth revolves round the sun preserving a distance of 93,000,000 miles. When we consider the size of the smallest atom, its orbit relatively speaking is by no means smaller than this distance, perhaps it is even greater. The planets residing in their infinitesimal skies have also their comparatively shorter and longer distances. It has already been stressed about the enormity of the distances between the planets and the boundless space of the planetary world, but nevertheless the very minuteness could also be described as infinitesimally small. As we have to work up to a number of twenty to twenty-five digits in our mathematical calculation for a prodigious vastness, so do we have to in assessing the minimum of an infinitesimal smallness. The number will be like a battalion in file. A famous astrologer, in describing the distances within which the minutest particles revolve round in the infinitesimally small sphere of the atom, has given us an example. He says that if one empties out the whole of Howrah station and then lets lose about five or six bees, one can then form some idea of the space that these molecules occupy. But to keep the few moving particles confined within the distance of a diffused space is the responsibility of the molecule's central substance that is working all the time with all its force. Otherwise the world of atoms would perish in no time, and all traces of this atom-made universe would be wiped out.

These minutest particles, even in a solid substance like gold, are separated by gaps. To quote the exact mathematical figure in describing these dimunitive gaps is not necessary as it would be only tiresome for the mind. But the question is why must there be gaps in the atoms? Why do they contain any gas? And why should there be liquid in them? The question is no different than when we ask how is it that the earth does not become attached to the body of the sun? Why does not the whole universe entangle itself into a huddled heap? The only answer is that, though drawn by the sun, the earth can keep at a distance because of its own rotating movement. If this movement hand been of sufficient strength, the earth, breaking its bond of pull, would have hurled itself into space. Or if there had been any lessening of the speed, it would have been then totally consumed by the sun. The gaps in the atoms exist because of this rotating movement. This is what resists the forces of attraction. Gaseous particles have greater speed. In such circumstances the body of atoms has to move at a speed that enables them to avoid meeting. They may sometimes collide but immediately they pull apart. The molecular attraction in the liquid is nominal so that the chance of their ever coming to close contact because of their speed is small. This magnetic pull is by far greater in a solid matter. The body of atoms lies confined in it within a restricted space. This does not mean that they are tranquil. A constant vibration runs through them, but their freedom of actions closely convergent. This throbbing movement in the atom is heat. As the agitation increases, the heat also becomes evident. It would be possible to keep them perfectly still if the heat could possibly be brought down to a temperature of 273 degrees centigrade below zero.

Let us now have a look into the compartment of a hydrogen atom.

Hydrogen is the lightest of all the gases. In the centre of its atom reigns only one electric charge which is called a proton, and drawn by its pull there is only one minute charge that revolves round it and is known as an electron. The proton is charged with electricity of the positive kind, while the electron is carrier of the negative kind. The negative electron is quick and moving, the positive proton is reticent and static. The weight of the electron is nominal, but the entire weight of the atom is practically contained in its central particle.

On the whole all electrons are of the negative kind except one which has been discovered to be of the positive kind, but it weighs the same as an electron. The kind of electron is known as a positron.

Sometimes it has been observed that some hydrogen atoms weigh twice as heavy as an ordinary one. After investigation it was found that the proton in the centre had a companion. We already know that the proton is positive-charged. Its companion at the centre when put to test appeared to be neutral-minded, belonging neither to a positive nor to a negative charge. It is therefore deprived of the essential virtue of electricity. Like its associate proton it weigh the same, but it is not capable of attracting the electron as the proton does, nor does it show any inclination to push out the proton. This electric spark is called a neutron. It has also been observed that no matter how heavy the standard weight of an atom may be with the addition of other grains, these neutral-minded sparks can never exert their influence on the electrons. Only one proton can keep one electron under control. As there is an increase in the number of protons at the centre of a molecule, there is also an equal number of electrons that they control. An oxygen-atom has eight protons at its centre. They are accompanied by eight neutrons, and the number of electrons revolving round them is exactly eight.

When these positives and negatives equal in number unite, there is harmony. But if in this regulated home a kind of disruption is caused by removing a few of the negatives, then according to the count of electricity there will be incongruity. The charge of the positive electricity will be far too great. When a home depending on the union of a man and woman has its feminine influence reduced, it generally follows that there is a dominance of the masculine power. It is the same in the molecules.

The word 'charge' is frequently used in connection with electricity. We do not find any restlessness in electricity in the things with which we come in contact in our everyday life. They are not charged, in other words they have in them an equal proportion of both kinds of electricity which are essential for preserving harmony. On the other hand, in any substance if one, ignoring its bond of agreement, supersedes the other, proclaiming its superiority, then we say matter is charged with electricity.

Let us rub any glass with a piece of silk. The result will be that some. electrons, due to the rubbing, will emerge from the glass and these will be transferred to the silk. Due to the lessening of these electrons the positive electricity will be in prominence in the glass. At the same time the negative electricity will increase in the silk. In other words, there will be a charge of negative electricity in the silk. The glass, having lost a few of its electrons, will have its positive charge drawing the piece of silk towards it. And again, the silk with its overwhelmingly surplus negatives will be drawn towards the glass. When the natural activities both in the silk and glass remain undisturbed, they are in their normal state of being and at rest within themselves. The existence of electricity is not even known in their state of tranquillity. But news of domestic discord spreads abroad as soon as an uneven distribution brings about a chaotic as soon as an uneven distribution brings about a chaotic state in electricity.

This applies in the case of a piece of glass or some similar substance when we remove a few electrons by just rubbing. If we ask the scientists the exact quantity of these electrons, they will undoubtedly tell us with a nod of their head that they may differ in number from anything between 300,000,000 and 600,000,000 according to the pressure of the rubbing. Crammed electrons rub one another as they pass through the filament, that is why an electric lamp lights up. The number of electrons that make this journey from one end to the other end of the filament is beyond all the calculations of mathematics. But this much is obvious, that the acute agitation in the atom controls itself by signing a bond of treaty with its positive and negatives, and that is why the universe retains such poise. A juggler beats the drum, and the tame-bear dances to its tune, showing us many a trick. If the juggler failed to beat the drum, and the tame bear, breaking its chains, ran at its own free will there would be chaos all around with its scratches and biting. There is also an invisible juggler who in his play and dance of creation is drumming a tune to make us follow its rhythm, subduing all the terrors and complexities that are within and outside us. In this conflict ridden creative ground these two players, coming to a mutual agreement, have turned this vast arena of all animate and inanimate beings into a place of fiery energy.

There are some scientists who, by comparing this world of atoms with the solar system, have said that body of electrons moved on different paths while wheeling round the central body in the molecule. There were other experts who proved to us that these rotating electrons jumped from the orbit into another and then returned again and again to their predestined paths.

A picture of the world of atoms as compared with the solar system shows that the positive electricity carrier is the atom's central substance, and the electrons revolve round it.

There is a barrier to accepting this theory. If the electron travelled on the same path continuously, it would gradually lose its energy, and narrow down its orbit until it would hit the central substance. This would be disastrous for the atom.

The opinion that has been confirmed today is that the electron does not travel on only one egg-shaped path but, on several. The distances of these orbits from the centre are fixed. No electron can pass through the last orbit nearest to the centre. It is only visible when it leaves its outer orbit to move on to the next. Why this happens and when it makes its sudden appearance have no fixed rules. The electron, by absorbing energy, jumps from its inner circuit to the outer one. Its jump varies according to the degree of energy that it reabsorbs. It scatters its energy only when it moves from its outer orbit to reach the inner. These sparks of scattered energy are what we receive as light. The electron could never diffuse energy if it kept moving on the same orbit. This is only an acceptable theory, there is no positive proof. It is when we accept this theory that we can explain how the atoms subsist, why the universe is not yet extinct.

Behind all these facets there is an abstruse truth, and we are a long way from understanding it. For the time being we can only bear this view in mind.

It has been mentioned before that the scientists, at one time, were very definite in announcing that the basic substance of the created world contained ninety-two primary elements. But at the evidence of the atoms the theory has since been disproved. And yet, they still hold the same titular honour. Once, all elementary substances had by reputation the property of being constant. No matter how they were split their behaviour would still remain unchanged. In the preliminary chapter of science it came to be seen that when they were split into their rudimentary state they contained two kinds of electric sparks moving together in rhythmic unison. All matter under the category of basic elements has retained its inherent behaviour because of these electric sparks that have united in a specific number. If this were the last word, their reputation would have remained intact, but an adverse testimony issued forth from their own group. There was an indication that although in lightweight atom the revolving movements of the electron and proton were regular throughout and constant, yet in a heavier atom the neutron and proton because of the overwhelming nature of their crowded proximity—like those in uranium and radium—were unable to protect their own treasure. Their main resources being constantly frittered away they would become lighter and lighter, changing form into another.

Until quite lately a basic element called Radium was hidden under its own gross covering. With its discovery the subtlest mystery of the molecules also came to be known. How the scientists first came to rely on their analysis is something that is worth remembering.

When the Roentgen ray was discovered it was found to have the power of penetrating a solid mass. At the time Henry Beckerel happened to be the professor of science in the Municipal School in Paris. He started an investigation to see if all self-luminous objects had this power of penetration. He collected a few of the elements and started his experiment. He wrapped them up in black paper and then laid them on a photographic plate. He found that Uranium was the only element that penetrated the black paper and left its mark on the plate. Thus the element with the heaviest of atoms was proved to be radio-active.

Uranium is extracted from a mineral substance called pitch-blende. Beckerel had a pupil, a highly intellectual woman, named Madame Curie. Her husband, Pierre Curie, was a professor at the Science Institute in Paris. Both husband and wife started a research on pitcblende, and found in it a radioactivity that was even more powerful than in uranium. There was a certain matter in pitchblende that caused this energy, and in discovering this, three other new metallic elements were detected—Radium, Polonium, and Actinium.

During their research forty other radio-active elements came to be known. Almost all of them were only recently discovered by science.

What appeared quite striking at the time was the strange behaviour of this new metallic element. While scattering its radio-grains from within, it turned itself into various rudimentary substance until it formed into lead. It seemed like some magic trick of science. In the list of their extravagance the first sparks that they emit are called Alpha according to the first letter of the Greek alphabet. They are small molecules of the positive kind. There are other sparks which they also throw off, and they are known as Beta. They are electrons, and as they are charged with negative sparks they have a tremendous speed. When an Alpha molecule falls into a passage as thin as a sheet of paper it is transformed into another state, it becomes helium gas. It takes more than that to thwart the speed of Beta molecules. Besides these two, the radium holds in its sheath yet another shaft called Gamma. It is not an atom or a fine molecule, it is a specific kind of ray. Its light, like the Roentgen ray, can pass through solid matter. The behaviour of these sparks is always the same in any circumstances, in the heat of melted iron, or in liquified gas. Moreover, nothing can make them revert to a state when they can form into solid grains again.

If without causing damage to the central nucleus of an atom a few electrons are removed from its body, there will be no doubt some deficiency in the allotted list of electricity, but such a blow will not be deadly. But the possibility of plunder in the private treasury of its central body will force the atom to change its face.

When the scientists gathered that there was no inherent unity within the atoms, they at first thought they would be able to apply the artillery-explosives of the radium to cause disorganization in the body of the atom, thus plundering its resources. But the aiming point was very subtle, identification was difficult, and after assailing it with numerous missiles, hardly one struck home. That is why, instead of depending on precarious war methods, the world today is busy building gigantic factories where a fantastically powerful radio-energy is being produced, by which the barriers of a nuclear fortification in the atom can be pierced through. A great champion of infallible strength keeps guard here. Today with the invention of the thousand-flamed missile that can destroy millions of people, workshops have also been set up side by side to experiment with atomic-explosives that can rend the impregnable heart of the most subtle substance of the universe.

It has already been mentioned that the Alpha ray loses its identity to become helium gas, which has been useful for us to verify the earth's age. When a certain quantity of helium gas is found on the stone of a mountain, by calculating the exact time it took to convert itself into gas, we are able to cast a horoscope of the mountain. By the same method the earth's age has also been estimated.

From the point of view of weight, the gas that occupies the immediate place above hydrogen is known as helium. It is a gas that has been very recently known among the scientists. It was first detected at a time of the sun's eclipse. Beyond the boundary of the periphery over millions of miles the sun spreads out its gauzy mantle of vaporous clouds, as the spring creates a mist round itself with water particles. When the sun is in eclipse we can see through a telescope the luminous gas that extends all around it. In English this far extensive gaseous light is known as Corona. In Bengali we may call it 'Kiritika'.

When in the year 1937 during a solar eclipse the opportunity was taken to examine this luminous gas, there appeared in its colour-chart three unknown white lines near its blue ray. The pundits came to the conclusion that perhaps an already known element had, through combustion, entered a different phase, and these lines were the indication. Or perhaps they were the message-carrier of entirely a new element. Nothing definite has been proved yet.

During the time of the 1868 eclipse the scientist were equally puzzled. The news came in a similar way of a hitherto unknown substance from the sun's gaseous border. This newly-found elementary matter was named helium, or 'of the sun'. For, at the time it was believed this gaseous matter was entirely a part of the sun. Thirty years passed when a famous physicist called Ramsay found in the earth's atmospheric air a mixture of this gas in a very small quantity. It was believed that this gas was rare on the earth. Later on it was discovered that the gas that came from the petroleum pits in North America contained a sufficient quantity of helium. It became easy then to utilize this gas. Up to this time, hydrogen, being considered very light in weight, served the purpose of fuel for airships. But though hydrogen was serviceable in flying, it was highly inflammable. It has caused destruction to many powerful dirigible balloon. There is no such furious burning propensity hidden in helium, and yet it is lighter than all the other gases except hydrogen. For the safety of an airship in the air this gas has therefore been very much in vogue. Even in medicine they have started using it for certain diseases.

It has been already said that matter with positive charge and matter with a negative charge attract each other, but particles with a similar charge repel each other. The nearer they are brought the fiercer is their repelling force. Similarly, when particles charged with different properties come close, their magnetic pull is also great. For this reason the electrons which are the nearest to the central substance travel much faster than the more distant ones in order to resist the greater magnetic pull. In the solar system the planets closer to the sun rotate with greater speed. More distant planets run a lesser risk as they move with comparative ease and modified speed.

The proton or electron has a diameter that is one fifty-thousandth part of that of an atom. This means that there is more empty space in an atom. If the atoms in the human body are pressed together tightly, they will occupy an almost invisible space of a dot.

In estimating the force of animosity between two protons, Professor Fedrick Sodey, a physicist, has stated that if one gramme of proton is placed on one pole of the earth and anther gramme on its opposite pole, the force of their resistance over this impermeable path will amount to a pressure of 49,200 lbs. If this is what happens then the fact that more than one proton can stay within the infinitesimal central space of the molecule in such proximity and yet be in harmony becomes difficult to understand. For, according to this rule the question crops up whether any matter could possibly survive beside one that had hydrogen as the sole property of the one supreme central proton in its atom. The whole universe would be then only composed of hydrogen gas.

On the other hand it can be seen that the metallic element uranium carries 92 protons and 146 neutrons. It certainly cannot control such a conglomeration, it gives out every now and again tiny sparks to lighten its central storage. As the burden is lessened to some extent, it is transformed into radium. When it is still lighter it becomes polonium. Ultimately it reaches stability by forming into lead.

One can easily express doubt as to how this stability can be attained at the price of shedding so much weight. After the sheddings are over, and making allowances for other deductions, eighty-two protons are still left in the possession of lead. How these protons with their natural antipathy for their own kind of positive sparks are able to keep peace in the atoms has not yet had an answers that is wholly satisfactory. Beyond the centre of the atom their quarrel persists, but within the centre they appear bound in friendship; this presents a difficult problem.

Instruments were made more powerful to suit the purpose of penetrating this mystery. Investigators induced a few more positive sparks to act against the aim of the atom's central protons. The force with which these sparks repelled them had a velocity of 6,720 miles a second. And yet the protons in the centre kept up their inherent virtue. They thwarted all the efforts of the offensive sparks. The driving force of the sparks was then increased. Scientists applied a resistant force with a velocity of 7,700 miles a second, but they were defeated in their pursuit. Eventually, after an on-slaught of a velocity of 8,200 miles a second, the defensive side showed signs of weakening. The attacking force, leaving its zone of dissipated energy, entered the centre fortification. It was detected that the space left between two similar-minded atoms, when all adverse tendencies come to terms, is many a millionth part of an inch. It follows then that within this narrowness of the atoms there is yet a great force stronger than the repelling force that exists between two protons, and this is of a magnetic kind. This force attracts the proton in the atom as well as the neutron. In other words, it exerts equal influence on matters whether they are charged with electricity or not. This great magnetic power dwelling in the heart of an atom has bound the whole universe into one. The controlling force that settles all domestic dissensions in the minute atom is the same force that sets the universe at rest.

A similar illustration can be drawn from our contemporary history. In China some of the generals in the army suppressing the Republican Government were determined to fight for a dictatorship by bringiing war and chaos to the country. If at the centre of this regime there had been a power stronger than all the reactionary forces at work, then there would have been unity in its administration which would have helped the political power to become healthy and free from danger. In the politics of the atom there is this force bigger than all the other forces, that is why whatever are reactionary by nature come to terms with it, and together they hold the peace of the universe. This makes us see clearly that the concord which we find in the universe is not the result of a placid docility. Out of all warring elements a powerful concord has been established. Those which individually are destructive, are the precursors of creation when united.

The chapter on radium is the most valuable in the history of the atoms, so that it needs a little elaboration. Radium is a metallic substance like iron and the rest. In size its atoms are large and heavy. Nobody knows why its atom bursts open and a small portion of it gets loose. In the Alpha ray that results from this breakdown of the molecule there is a flow of small particles, each of which is made in conjunction with two protons and two neutrons. In other words, they are in uniformity with the central body of the helium atom. The Beta ray has only a flow of electrons. The Gamma ray contains no such particles. It is the same type as light. Why such disintegration must take place has not yet been found out. Because of this waste, however small it may be, the radium atom does not keep its previous form. It changes in its behaviour. The Alpha particles by exhausting two electrons change their fate, turning into helium gas. This process of ejection can neither be hampered nor aggravated from the outside. Whether the surrounding condition is hot or cold, whether it co-operates with or merges into other molecules or not—in other words without depending on any external influence—the radium atom starts its process of disintegration within itself. On average the age of the atom is 2,000 years, but its dislodged grain from which the Alpha ray issued forth has only four days to live. After this, more splitting takes place until it reaches the state of lead. When the Alpha ray starts shooting out it keeps up a speed of 10,000 miles a second. But when it passes through any solid substance or even through air, it eases its pace by the time it covers a distance of two to three inches. The Alpha ray moves directly in a straight line. How this is possible is rather thought provoking, because a helium molecule is much lighter and smaller than an oxygen or nitrogen atom in the air. It has to push itself through multitudes of much heavier atoms thronging the space of those three inches. It is not like pushing through a crowd, it is like penetrating a solid mass. What we understand by an atom is that there is the central body, and surrounding it there are revolving electrons. To break through such a formation of guards a tremendous moving force is needed. The Alpha ray seems to possess such force. It can easily pass through different orbs. While passing through other atoms it brings havoc. Perhaps it may make an atom lose its electron. Then gradually there will be two or three more dislodged electrons. And they, losing their link, will wander about, though not for long. They will soon become attached to other atoms. Thus the atom that loses its electrons will acquire a positive charge, and the atom that seizes the lost electrons will be negatively charged. And if by chance they are sufficiently near, they will be equal once again through mutual exchange. When the disparity is settled the natural imbalance in electricity ceases. Usually the helium atom has two electrons. But when it issues forth out of radium as an Alpha ray and rushes through other matter, its two electrons at the same time become disrupted. Afterwards, when the hurdle is over, this deficiency is rectified through other dislodged electrons, so that it can regain its natural state.

One more thing must be added. The electrons, protons and neutrons are the same in all matter; the difference lies in the way they are distributed. The molecule containing six positive-minded protons in total forms into carbon, in other words it is an atom of carbon variety. The atom of nitrogen has seven electrons. The oxygen atoms has eight. There is only one electron in the atom of hydrogen, but uranium has ninety-nine. The atoms fall into their different caste-groups according to the number of positive protons they happen to possess. In the cadence of numerical difference lies the diversity of creation.

While working on rays, the scientists were upset in their

calculations by the sudden appearance of an unknown energy. Its radiation was named the cosmic ray. It could be called the incidental ray. Where it came from it could not be found, but it was present every where. There is not a single thing in the whole world either animate or inanimate—that does not feel its direct touch. It sends its shafts even through the atoms of a hard metallic substance spurring it on. Perhaps it is helping existence towards life-force, or maybe towards annihilation—but which we do not know for certain. What we are sure of is its power.

This cosmic radiation showers upon us unceasingly though is sources still remain veiled in mystery. What we know is that tremendous is its energy, its circulating power covers the entire sky, it has entry into each and every substance, whether on land, in air or water. Science has its spy constantly watching this great adventitious visitor. One day, who knows, the secret of its origin may be divulged.

Many hold the opinion that this cosmic ray cannot be anything but light, and that it is many times more forceful than the Roentgen ray. This is why it is capable of passing through solid lead or a sheet of gold. We know from the scientists' investigations that the ray contains radio-active particles. Wherever there is a stronger magnetic force in the world, it is attracted by it; when shifting its line of path it concentrates its power on the cardinal points. That is the reason why we find its rays assemble in varying degree in different parts of the earth.

Varied opinions are still astir regarding the cosmic ray. Since the new discovery of the atom there has been no end to activities in the scientific field of many exploring minds with their different theories. In the universal workshop of fundamental laws any sure sign of irrevocability has been impossible to find. If there is any such inviolability it can only be claimed by the one primeval energy, which is the preface to everything that exists, and through the manifold stages of manifestation of which the universe has built up its diversities.

2

Through millions and millions of years,
The stars shine,
Fiery whirlpools revolve and rise
In the dark ever-moving current of time.
In that current
The earth is a bubble of mud;
Within it, this life
In its infinitesimally small duration,
With a tiny speck of flame,
Offers its worship to the Infinite.
But for this,
The vast temple of the universe
Would be empty of the echoing sound of a conch,
There would be no wayfaring pilgrim.
Light with its adoring chant becoming voiceless
Would be ever silenced.

THE WORLD OF STARS

We have had so far a glimpse of the formless world of energy that permeates the universe. It is through the assembly of energy that the world of forms manifests itself in the stars and planets.

It is better to say from the beginning that we can never really get a true picture of the existing universe. So little of it comes within our view. Besides, our eyes, ears and the other organs of our perception have their own characteristics. Therefore all the objects of the universe appear before us in a particular way taking particular forms. A wave hits our eyes and we see light. But if the wave be either more subtle or more dense we are blind. What we see is but a little, by far the major part remains unseen. We hear and see just enough to suit our purpose of living. Nature shows no keen interest in the idea that we may become scientists. Man's eyes do the work of both telescope and microscope but in a small degree. If our senses had a wider range, or the nature of our senses were of a different kind then our world would also have been a different one.

Such a different world has indeed come to be realized by scientists. The difference is so great that in the knowledge of it our language of everyday living becomes of little use. There is such a steady growth of technical terms in our vocabulary that the ordinary man finds them difficult to understand.

Man once came to the conclusion that in the universal globe the earth's seat was immovable, that the sun star revolved round it. For such a conclusion he could not be blamed, for he had only his normal eyes for seeing the earth. Today his eyesight has expanded, he has developed eye for a greater vision to see the universe. He has been made to accept that it is the earth that is not still, that it revolves round the sun, spinning round and round like a Dervish in his dance. Its path is long; to cover the path it takes a little more than 365 days. There are other planets with yet longer courses, to cover which they take such a long time that a man's whole span of life would have to be increased in order to live through this period.

Sometimes we find the night sky smeared with clusters of stars, filled with light. They are known as Nebulae. In a nebula there are some very light, far-extensive gaseous clouds and congregations of stars as well. It is known with the help of telescopes and cameras that the number of stars amassed in the crowded nebulae totals many a million; they move with incredible speed. The question is how then is it possible for these multitudes of stars to avoid collision and not be shattered to pieces while they move within the orb of a nebula with such speed? To describe these numbers of stars as 'multitudes' is perhaps wrong. For there is no crowding together or rubbing of shoulders amongst these stars. Keeping a good distance from one another each travels its lone journey. Sir James Jeans, as he described the distances between the different revolving electrons in a molecule, also drew a similar comparison regarding the planets in their orbits. Waterloo is a big station in London, which is no doubt much bigger than Howrah station in Calcutta. He said that if we emptied out the whole of Waterloo station and scattered there half a dozen dust grains, then the gaps between these separated grains could compare in a relative sense with the distance in the clustering stars in the sky. He said that no matter how formidable the size and number of the stars might be, they were insignificant compared with the measureless void of the sky.

The scientists think that in the beginning, long before there was any sign of diversity of form in creation, there was an all-pervading burning gas through-out. All hot objects have a natural tendency to diffuse heat. Boiling water comes out at first in the form of gas. As it gets cooler and cooler the vapour condenses into drops of water. 'Even solid matter when considerably heated will gradually turn into gas. In a similarly heated condition all matters of the universe, whether heavy or light, were once in a gaseous state. For millions of years, from age to age, this burning gas has been cooling off gradually. As the heat gradually lessened small matter of solidified grains became detached from the gas. The innumerable grains thus formed crowded together in the shape of stars, creating a nebula. Our sun is a star included in one of these nebulae.

A huge telescope has been set up on the peak of an American mountain through which one of the largest nebulae is visible. It is among the clusters of stars named Andromeda. This nebula looks almost like a carriage wheel in shape, and it revolves. To complete its circuit once, it takes about 20,000,000 years. Its light takes 9,000,000 years to reach the earth.

The distance between the nearest star and us—a star which we may call our neighbour in the starry area—is such that it would be difficult to explain by merely arranging digits. We can understand a distance by a numerical figure when it concerns something that is within our circumscribed earth, and which we can actually assess moving along by car, train or ship. But stepping outside the earth, as soon as we reach the abode of the stars, the language of figures sounds like a madman's ravings. In the mathematical calculations regarding stars a number seems to lay digit after digit like a highly prolific insect on the earth.

Usually we measure distances either by miles or a croash (every two miles). If we applied the same method in the case of the stars, mathematics would be a burdensome problem. The sun is distant enough from us, but these groups of stars are even more distant, many a million times further away. To calculate these distance would be like counting thousands and thousands of sovereigns in terms of 'cowries'. Man has lessened his burden of writing by introducing numerical figures; he does not have to draw a thousand lines in order to write a thousand. But in the calculations of the astrological world this terms of reference was found inadequate, so that a new method of reference has been invented. This can be described as measurement by light's movement. During a year counted as 365 days, light travels, 5,800,000,000,000 miles. As the sun's revolution is counted by

365 days as a solar year, so the movements of the stars, their size and the frontiers of their jurisdiction are counted by so many light years. Our world of stars has a diameter measuring about 100,000 light years. There are other worlds of stars, many a hundred thousand more, outside our own world of stars. Among these alien worlds of stars one has revealed its identity on our photographic plate. It has been calculated that it is nearly 50,000,000 light years away from us. The distances between our neighbouring star and ourselves is 25,000,000,000,000 miles. From this we can understand the immensity of the space in which our universe sails. People tell us today that we have wars because of the shortage of space in our world. If there had been the slightest space-restriction where the stars are concerned, there would have been a chaotic collision bringing the universe to a fatal end.

After the age of the eyes, there followed the age of the telescope. With the increasing power of the telescope, our vision of the heavenly worlds also widened. Where we found gaps before, we now saw swarms of stars. There are though many gaps which still remain unfilled. That is not surprising. There are other worlds of stars than our own whose light is beyond the range of our telescopic sight. Man's eyes were defeated when with the help of a telescope he hoped to detect a ray whose radiance was no more than the flame of a lamp burning at 8.575 miles away. The telescope brings a messaage to the eyes according to its capacity. If the eyes, in return, fail to possess the power to carry this flickering news into the region of understanding, what other means can be of avail! But the light-capturing power of a photographic plate has much more durability than the eyes can register. Science set up this power for use. To cast its net into the furthermost sky it applied photography. It installed such photographic instruments as were able to serve a warrant of light on the deep-covered face of darkness. The telescope with photography, and photography with colour-chart appliances were combined. Recently this strength has been amplified to a rare degree. The various substances in the sun are burning gases. When they appear mingled as they are, it becomes impossible to sift them out for close examination. For this reason an American scientist tried and invented a telescopic apparatus for the observation of the sun, by which each coloured ray from the assembled light of the burning gases could be separated, and by its help we were able to see this particular gaseous form of the sun. It is by seeing the sun freely and separately in the colour of either burning calcium or burning hydrogen that we came to know a great deal about the activities in its gaseous conflagration which in no other way has been possible.

When the white light is divided into its seven separate rays, the red lies on one extremity and the violet on the other. There are other rays that extend beyond them which we do not see.

The wave length of the indigo ray measures a 15,000,000th part of an inch. In other words, the wave that is raised in this coloured ray has this measurement taken from one crest to the crest of the following wave. There are 15,000,000 waves in a distance of an inch. The red ray has waves that are twice as long. When the red glow in a burning piece of lead gradually becomes dim and then can no longer be seen, there still remain within it big waves of unseen rays that keep recurring. If they had the power of freshening up our eyesight, we would see their retreating glow still in the extinguished lead. Similarly, in the dust of a summer evening after the sun has disappeared we would still see the retreating red-glow of the summer-hot earth, whereby the earth would be still visible to us.

There is no absolute darkness. What we do not see also contains light. Even the dark deepening skies beyound the world of stars have various rays that are shining all the time. It is by the aggregate help of a colour-chart, telescope and photograph that we are able to bring even these invisible couriers within the canvas of our visibility, and force out of them their own secrets.

The ray that is on the outer border of the violet ray not so useful to the scientists as the dark-hidden ray outside the red ray.

The reason is that any ray of a shorter wave-length loses a lot of itself in crossing the earth's atmospheric air. These rays are not good as messengers of the far distant worlds. They are the informers of the atomic world. The atom when heated to a particular point vibrates with white light. With further increase in the heat we see a light that is on the out-skirts of the violet ray. Ultimately when the very central substance of the molecule is affected, waves of much shorter length are caused by that great agitation, and these are known as Gamma rays. Man has strengthened the power of his instruments to such an extent that he is able to use rays like the X-ray and Gamma ray.

What it amounts to is that man, by the aid of a colour-chart determined by a telescope and photograph, has brought the distant unseen world of the starry region within the scope of our horizon. We have come to know the existence of other worlds of stars beyond our own starry world. What is more, the fact that these stars, whether in our sky or in the skies beyond, are themselves revolving simultaneously has also been detected by the eyes of these instruments.

When in the distant sky a luminous mass of gas which we call a star either approaches us or recedes from us, it affects our eyesight in a particular way. If it were a fixed object, the amount of wavelengths that it would have sent out touching our sensitivity would be in our opinion much less when it came nearer, and much more when it receded further. The rays having shorter wavelengths tend towards the violet in the seven rays of light, and those which have longer wavelengths approach nearer to the red. So that a chart indicating different coloured signals tells us when the star comes nearer or gets further away from us. When a train whistling passes by, we find its sound has at that moment a much harsher note. The reason is that the echoing whistle strikes our ears by raising a certain number of sound-waves in the air, and these soundwaves when the train comes nearer, are drawn together as they hit our ears, giving us the impression of an intensified note. The intensity in the seven-rayed is towards the violet ray.

Some of the gaseous nebulae have a brilliance that is not their own. They are illumined by the galaxy of stars that are crowded within them. Then again, there are times when the molecule of the nebulae absorb the light of the stars, and then transform it into rays of a different wave-length.

There is another characteristic about a nebula. It is smeared in places with dark patches that look like clouds—they are the black gaps in the thickly populated clusters of stars. According to the investigations of the scientist Bernard, there are almost two hundred of these dark patches in the sky. He thinks that they are opaque gaseous clouds; they hide the stars underneath them. Some of them are near, some are at a distance, some are small, some are prodigiously large.

If we try to measure the density of all the crowded matter that is scattered over the subservient parts of our starry sky, we find it is very small. There are only half a dozen atoms in the densest inch. We realize how small indeed the number is when we compare it with the fact that in a research laboratory when a vacuum is created by the fiercest of pumps, there still remain many millions of molecules in its densest inch.

Our own world of stars is a huge, flat and elliptical world that wheels round and round, and is studded with many hundreds of millions of stars. In between the stars the sky is filled with fine gas—in some places it is rarefied, in some dense, in other places bright and in some very opaque. The sun is situated in a starry cloud, and its distance from the centre of the world of stars is about one-third of its diameter. The stars crowd together more towards the centre of a nebula.

The star Antares had a diameter of 390,000,000 miles, and the diameter of the sun is 864,000 miles. The sun is considered to be an average-sized star. There are many other worlds of stars more many thousands, besides our own world of stars compared to which the sun is but a very mediocre star. Encompassing all these there is this universe, the limit of which we do not know.

The sun with all its planets is ever revolving, and with it

all the stars in the wheeling circle are also revolving simultaneously, pivoting round one centre. The speed of the sun's rotating motion in this region is about 200 miles per second. The sun would have been thrown off by its own motion from the background of these wheeling stars like shot-out particles from the wheels of a running vehicle, but the thousands of millions of stars do not allow it to step out of bounds.

The fact of this magnetic pull must be common knowledge to everybody, but in describing the universe it cannot be excluded.

There is a story prevalent that the great scientist Newton one day saw an apple fall to the ground which immediately raised a question in his mind. He wondered why it must fall down and not fly upwards. Many other questions were also troubling his mind. He tried to think what it was that made the moon revolve round the earth, and what attracted the earth to rotate round the sun. The incident of the apple gave him the idea that the earth must have a magnetic force, it was drawing everything else towards itself. If it were so, why must the moon be then an exception? Surely, all things whether far or near must come within the sphere of the earth's attraction! The idea gradually spread. The conclusion was that it was not the earth alone, but everything was drawing everything else. According to the weight of each matter it exercised its own magnetic pull. Besides there was an increase or decrease in this magnetic pull as the distance grew greater or narrower. When the distance is twice as much the pull is four times less. And when the distance grows four times the descrease in the pull is sixteen times. If it were not not so, all the resources of the earth would have been plundered away by the sun through its magnetic pull. In the wrestling match between magnetic forces the earth remained a winner over its neighbours. About seventy years after Newton's death there was another English scientist, Lord Cavendish, who hung up two leaden balls in his laboratory and gave visible proofs how they attracted each other according to the specified rules. Conforming to these rules, even I am drawing every little thing that is on my table as I sit writing. The earth, the moon, the sun and every one of the stars in the wide universe, or even the dimunitive and that is creeping near me in search of food I am drawing towards me. The ant, in return, is drawing me also, though needless to say I am not in the least worried by it, nor have I caused the ant the slightest anxiety because of my pull. There are many inconveniences though, due to the earth's force of gravity. For the purpose of walking we have to raise our feet, but the earth forces them down. We get out of breath when we have to cover a long distance, and the time we take is also unnecessarily long. Trees and plants greatly benefit by the result of this gravitational force, but with human beings it is a different story. And that is why man has to wrestle with this force from the day he is born till the day he dies. He would have flown long ago, but the earth has been reluctant to let him leave its soil. Man had to invent gadgets and machinery in order to free himself from this constant pull of the twenty-four hours. He could in this way bluff the earth to some extent, though not wholly. But we have to bow down to this force when we realize that if ever the earth slackens its hold on us we shall be in no time flung off the earth's surface into the void—nobody knows where—because of the speed of its revolving motion. As a matter of fact, the force of gravity on the earth is such that we are able to walk, and yet we cannot leave the earth.

Thus the world that issued forth from the union of two molecular sparks of contradictory nature is seen to possess two opposing activities prevalent throughout—motion and pull, freedom and restriction. On the one side is the eternal movement of the universe, and on the other is the eternal pulling force of the universe. Everything is pulling as well as moving simultaneously. What this movement is, from where it issues forth is not known. Moreover, what this magnetic force is and from where it originates, is equally unknown. In science today, the materiality of a substance has become a slender thing; what is found to be strong and prevalent is this movement and the force of resistance. If there were only movement, moving would be one straight line into infinity. But this force of a pull brings it within an encircling space, makes it rotate within an orbit. A gap of many thousands of miles exists between the sun and the planets. A bodiless magnetic force with its invisible reins from across this emptiness of void is ever causing the planets to move round and round like circus-horses. Simultaneously the sun is also revolving at the pull of a great luminary wheel made of millions of stars all in motion. Looking at the universe pivoting on its axis we find the same rhythmic play of an endless pull and motion. In the world of the atoms the distance between a proton and its electrons, relatively speaking, is the same as that compared to the distance between the sun and planets. The same magnetic force crossing space is also causing the groups of electrons to wheel round eternally on their destined orbits. Whatever exists, is because it retains an endless harmony between speed and restraint. It should be mentioned here that the pull between a proton and elctron is not of magnetic attraction, it is of radio-activity quality. The pull within the atom is of radio-active, but the pull from outside is the force of gravity. Just as man's pull in his own home is of relationship, but the pull outside is of the ties of society.

This theory of a gravitational force has been current since the time of Newton. We have come to believe that there is an invisible force of attraction between all objects, no matter what the intervening space is.

But there is some obstacle to presenting such a picture. The gravitational force loses no time in acting. It has been already mentioned that light takes time to cross the outer space before it can reach us. The radio-active energy also sends out waves as it passes through space. But in the case of the force of gravity, in spite of many investigations, it was never established that it loses time in motion. Its impact is immediate. Moreover, what is still more amazing is that this magnetic force heeds no impediment in its course of action as light or heat does. No matter what object you hang up in the air, and what obstacles you put in between the object and the earth, its pressure is never less. Its behaviour is unlike any other forces.

Eventually Einstein proved to us that this gravitational force is not a force at all. We live in a world where by the very nature of its shape each object is forced to lean towards another object. All matter surrounded by its own vacuum has its inverse virtue whose manifestation is in the gravitational pull. It is omnipresent, it is without change. Even light has to conform to these rules of a concave universe. The proofs have been many. The picture of a magnetic force was simple from the point of view of understanding, but this new geometry by the aid of which we are able to calculate the exact leanings of this concave vacuum can only be within the grasp of a very few.

If what we understand by gravitational pull be described as 'spherical gravity', the complexity of the problem may perhaps disappear.

Our world of stars is like an island in the immense vacuum of the sky. We can see many other islands of stars scattered in remote distances. Among all these islands the nearest one to us is seen close to the groups of stars called Andromeda. It looks like a rather hazy star. Its light that we see today began its journey about 900,000 years ago. There are yet other wheel-like nebulae whirling into coils which are even farther away. It has been calculated that the one farthest amongst them is situated at a distance of 300,000,000 light years. The total number of these worlds of stars with all their congregations of millions of stars cannot be less than a thousand million.

There has been a surprising conjecture lately that all these worlds of stars, barring the nearest two or three are constantly moving away from our world. The further away they go, the greather is their speed. Some pundits have come to conclude that the universe encompassing the aggregate worlds of stars that we know of, is gradually swelling. So that with the swelling of the universe the distance between the constellations of stars are also increasing. They are moving away at such speed that the distances between them will be double what they are now in 1,300,000,000 years. In other words, the worlds of stars would be double the size in the time the earth took to reach its globular form.

What is more, in the opinion of a group of scientists, the sky with its spherical form is also expanding with the matter-ridden universe. In their opinion if a line is drawn from a point in the sky, it will revolve back to the same original point at some time instead of proceeding eternally. What it amounts to is this, that all the worlds of stars are in the orb of the sky as all life—man, beast and vegetation—clings to the globe of the earth. So that if the worlds of matter do swell up, it must be in proportion to the expansion of the spherical sky. But it is better to bear in mind that this has not been yet an accepted theory. The sky is infinite, time is everlasting, and this opinion still holds good. In speaking about the sky, whether it all bubbles or not, our Shastras say that all this creation proceeds towards annihilation and out of this annihilation a new creation is hinted at, like sleep alternating waking. From time unknown creation and destruction like day and night take their turn, and keep recurring. There is no beginning, there is no end—this is easier to imagine.

In the constellation of Posius there is a bright star named Algel. It has a steady glow for sixty hours. Then within the next five hours its brightness diminishes by one-third. It starts getting bright again. It regains its whole brightness after five hours, and its full richness lasts for sixty hours. This change in its radiation is caused because of its companion star. It is in eclipse and out of eclipse alternately as it revolves round.

There is another group of stars whose brilliance does not depend on any outside cause, but due to some inward tidal flow and ebb it increases or decreases. The star remains expanded for a few days at a stretch, and then shrinks to a smaller size. Its light appears to throb like a heart-beat. These stars were first found in the constellation of Cypheus and hence are called cypodes. Their discovery has helped a great deal towards measuring distances in the worlds of stars.

There is yet another group of stars worthy of mention, and they are called new stars. Their light all of a sudden becomes conspicuously bright, increasing from many thousands to many hundreds of thousands of times. Then it gradually gets dim again. During the time these stars flared-up, becoming visible, it was thought to be their first appearance, and accordingly they were named new stars.

Some time ago, close to the constellation of Lacerta, one such new star shone excessively bright. It discharged one after another four layers of rays. These freed sparks, it was observed, had a speed of 2,200 miles a second. This star is at a distance on 2,600 light years from us. In other words, these flakes of burning gas that flew out of the star and came within our sight was an incident that happened 650 years before the birth of Christ. What has been the fate of these discarded flakes is still a matter of conjecture. Did they become quite detached, and breaking all bonds with the star disappear into the great void, or losing all lustre and drawn by its pull did they turn into mere satellites? From this instance, that there could be such a flare-up in the star, some pundits have come to estimate that perhaps these masses of gaseous flames torn out of the body of a star are the origin of the planets. Perhaps, at one time the sun conforming to the ethics of a new star frittered away portions of itself, thus giving birth to its planet-sons. Following this argument it seems also possible that every ancient star must have gone through this process of explosion, creating thereafter a dynasty of planets. Probably there is hardly a place in the sky for many barren stars.

There is another opinion that when an outward moving star gets caught in the magnetic sphere of another star, it causes this havoc. How far this opinion affects the origin of the earth we shall discuss later.

We have, in our world of stars, different kinds of stars. Some send out rays that are a thousand times brighter than the sun, some are one hundredth part less bright. Some are densely packed, and some are thinly sparsed. The surface-heat in some amounts to 20,000° or 30,000° Centigrade while in other it is not more than 3,000° Centigrade. Some have a habit of contracting and expanding, causing ebb and flow in their light. Some travel a lonely path while others move in pairs which make up one-third of the total number of the stars. Being caught up in the net of the magnetic whirl these paired-off stars go through their revolutionary rounds. The burden of revolving round falls on the one that happens to be the weaker of the two. As in the instance of the sun and the earth. The feebler earth has, no doubt, its magnetic pull, but it is not enough to shake the sun. The act of rotating is being accomplished by the earth alone. When two luminary bodies are equal in strength they have between them a common centre of aim round which they both rotate.

We hear different theories about how these stars came to pair off originally. Some say there is robbery at the root of it. In other words, true to the maxim that force is strength, one came to imprison the other, making it its companion. The other theory is that a star becomes two out of its own body. The explanation is this. When a star gets cooler and cooler it becomes more and more compact. As density takes place it whirls all the faster. In the momentum of this speed its expelling force also mounts up. Because of this expelling force, when a carriage wheel moves at a great speed it flings out dirt or dust that may be attached to it, and moreover if the joints of the wheel happen to be rather weak, some parts are bound to come loose and shoot forth. With the revolving speed still increasing and its force of expulsion getting stronger the wheel at some time will break into two. In the case of a star these two parts, becoming two stars from that moment, star on their united journey.

Some of these paired-off stars take many thousands of years to complete one round of their revolution. Sometimes it is seen that as they revolve, the one keeps the other hidden from our view, and is a hindrance to its brightness. But this damage to brightness would matter little unless the shadowing star was no brighter than the other. The degree of brightness varies a great deal from star to star. There are stars that are completely devoid of lustre. Stars which once started life with tremendous size and fierce burning heat cooled down long before they had lived out three-quarters of their existence, having frittered away all the stored resources of their energy. In their old age these stars, being insolvent, retired into the infamy of darkness.

There is a star of a gigantic size called Beteljeus. We can see from its red light that it is an aged star. And yet its sparkle is vivid. It is a great distance away, its light reaching the earth in 190 years. What is more it is of a tremendous size; its body can accommodate many millions of suns. Then again there is another star in the constellation of Brishchic called Antares, which is double the size of Beteljeus. Besides these, there are stars which, though filled with gas, have solid matter that weighs heavier than lead.

It does not follow that these gigantic stars are of such enormous size because they possess great solidity of matter, they just swell up to such a state. On the other hand, there are many stars which are small because their gaseous total is reduced to a bundle-tight mass. The density of the sun is somewhere in between. In other words, it is a little more than that of water. The star Capella has, on an average, a density equivalent to our atmospheric air. But if we did go there for a change of air we would be landed there in an atmosphere that would differ from ours vastly. The change will be greater still in the case of the red-hued demon-star Beteljeus in the constellation of Orion, and the star Antares in the galaxy of Brishchic. Their density is so thin that they hardly resemble anything that exists on the earth. It is even thinner than the air-pumped rarefied gas found in a research laboratory.

Then again there are white-coloured dwarf stars. Their density is such that it even exceeds lead or platinum. Yet they are not congealed, they are of the same gaseous body as the sun-family is made of. There is such tremendous burning heat in their interior that the electrons are disrupted from the bonds of their protons, they are released from the burden of revolving round. The distance that is necessary for preserving their mutual respect is narrowed down, so that there is constant clashing in the broken-down, disintegrated atom. As the space in the atom is dwarfed, the star also gets dwarfed accordingly. At the same time, due to such irregular activities threatening the peace of the atom, the heat increases more and more beyond its natural state. The thick gas becomes heavier in weight, about 3,000 times heavier than platinum. This is why the dwarf stars are small in size, but not less in heat, and at their maximum they even surpass a giant star in weight. The star Cyrius has a companion star that is rather hazy. It is small in size like an ordinary planet. And yet its total substantial weight is as much as that of the sun. The density of the sun is a little less than one and a half times that of water. The companion star of Cyrius has a density that is on the whole 50,000 times more than that of water. Its gaseous matter filling the size of a matchbox will weigh more than 4,100 lbs. On the other hand, the same quantity of matter in the very small companion star of Perseus will weigh more than 820,000 lbs. We have been hearing recently that this opinion is not upheld by some scientists. In the beginning when the earth was going through the process of being formed and moulded there was a constant contradiction between the land and water. Where there was a cave one day, there was a mountain the next day. For a while this was the consistent state in natural science. There was no end to opinions that were once prominent and later lost their significance.

In our starry world the stars pursue different paths, some proceeding toward the east and some to the west. The sun is travelling at the rate of 200 miles a second. There is a giant star whose racing speed is 700 miles a second. And yet what is miraculous is that none of them steps out into the void disregarding the rules of their world. Gathering millions of stars within the great ensnaring net of a curve the world is spinning round and round like a top. There are other distant worlds of stars beyond our world of stars, and they are caught into the same whirlpool of revolution. Similarly, in the region of infinitesimally small atoms, there is also the same whirling motion of the electrons and protons. Round this ever-revolving speed of so many luminous worlds flows the current of time. That is why we have described the universe in our language as 'jagat'—that which has cognition because it moves—in movement it has its origin, and to move is its inherent tendency.

However awe-inspiring we may find this immense magnitude in speed distance and the measure of time regarding the worlds of stars, the inconceivable force, and the circumferences of their fiery revolving movements, we have yet to admit that what is still more miraculous is that man is aware of them, and surmounting all necessities of life he is ever eager for knowledge of them. Smaller than small, perishable at any moment is his body. His presence occupies only a momentary corner in the history of the universe; a tiny spot in the vast universe that is ever turning is where he dwells, and yet he keeps an account of the immense, the immeasurable and the formidable subtleties of a universe closing on infinity. There is no other splendour than this in the world, or perhaps, who knows. there may be in the profusion of creation, some other world, which conquering the heart of another matter is expressing itself in some other form. But what man has proved is that the supreme is not in outward form, not in weight but in inward fulfilment.

3

The sun of the first day
Asked a question
At the new appearance of
Existence....
'Who are you?'
It received no reply.
Years came and went by,
The sun at the day's end,
Asked its last question,
As it set on the western shore
Of the ocean,
In evening's stillness....
'Who are you?'
It had no reply.

THE SOLAR WORLD

When we try to consider the tie of relationship between the sun and the planets, we find that the revolutionary path of the planets lies almost in the same area as the sun's equator. This is one fact. There is the other that the sun as it revolves on its own axis moves in a direction that is similar to that of the planets which move round the sun all the while simultaneously. We can gather from this that the sun's relationship with the planets is an hereditary one. Let us see how the question of heredity comes in.

The stars are revolving round keeping a distance of many millions of miles from one another, so that the question of their coming into very close contact or clashing into one another is practically impossible. Some have guessed roughly that about 2,000,000,000 years ago such an incident of an unforeseen nature did take place. A big star came very close to the sun at that period. Due to the magnetic pull of the star there were tidal waves of gaseous fire that swelled up with a tremendous force in the sun and the visiting star as well. Some of the waves, as they mounted up higher and higher in the pressure of pull, became detached and flew off. The huge star did perhaps appropriate some of them, but the rest, drawn by the great pull of the sun, began to revolve round it. As they lost their heat, they became divided again into smaller sections. These bigger and smaller sections of gaseous flames are the origin of the planets. Gradually becoming cooler by emitting heat they took the form of planets. One of them is the earth. From the distances of the stars, their number and speed, it has been calculated that such an accident may occur again in about 50,000,000,000 or 60,000,000,000 years. If one accepts this theory of the origin of the planets, one has to admit that the attendant planets which have been thus created out of a star are rare incidents in the universe. But as the boundary of the elliptical universe is steadily widening, with the result that the stars are getting farther and farther away from one another, this also must be admitted, that in those former days when the range of the globular sky was much narrower, there must have been constant collisions between one star and another. It also stands to reason that during those periods of hustled meetings of the stars, it was possible that many a star became disrupted and planets were born out of their own dislodged fragments. We also have to accept according to our present calculation, a condition under which our sun must have been hit by other suns in those days when the universe was much less expanded. Those who are of a different opinion say that in a particular stage of development in a star a time arrives sooner or later when it bursts open like the ripe fruit of the silk-cotton tree, scattering flaky clusters of burning gas which revolve round in great force. Such burning gas has been actually seen to come out of certain stars. There was a very small star which could not be seen distinctly without the help of a telescope a few years ago. At one time it suddenly became radiant, almost vying with the other bright stars in the sky. A few months later it again lost the brilliance of its power to such an extent that it could not, as before, be seen without the help of a telescope. The fact that during this restricted bright period to the star, it emitted clusters and clusters of burning gas, and that these becoming solidified as they cooled, could give rise to planets and their satellites, is a theory that is not so incongruous to imagine. Conforming to this opinion one can conclude that millions of stars have gone through this stage of development and, therefore, the universe is filled with billions of worlds of stars with their own groups of satellite-planets like those in the solar system. If the nearest star to us happens to have its own group of planets we are not able to see it, for such a powerful telescope has not yet been discovered.

Quite recently a young scientist in Cambridge named Littleton has expounded a new theory about the origin of the solar world. It has already been stated earlier that there are stars which go in pairs, and rotate round one another. In his opinion the sun was one of a pair. A wandering luminary in its revolutionary round came to collide with the sun's companion-star and hurled it to a great distance. While resuming its journey, due to the magnetic pull of both, a huge layer of vapourous flame was forced out of it. In it there was a mingling of substances from both. A part of this vapourous thread was drawn within the circuit of the sun's magnetic force. Our groups of planets originated from this ensnared gaseous flame. Being small in size they did not take long to cool; as they began to cool the gaseous masses at first turned liquid. Then losing more and more heat there came a time when they solidified.

It is well to remember that these are surmises, and are no sure proofs.

It is important to mention that the sun is entirely filled with gas. All the substances that the earth is made of—solid metal, stone and earth—are also in the sun but in a tremendously heated gaseous state. The imprints on a spectrometer have proved this to us.

A nebula has a thin covering of gas which has been mentioned before. The more we penetrate within this covering, the more dense we find the gas and the heat more intense. The surface heat of the sun measures $10,000^0$ Fahrenheit. As we enter deeper into it, we reach a layer where the hard-pressed gas loses all transparency. The heat there measures $15,000,000^0$ Fahrenheit. Finally we come to the centre having a temperature of $72,000,000^0$ Fahrenheit. Here the sun maintains a physical body that is more solid than hard stone or iron, and yet potentially it is gas.

Let us fall back on an imaginary description rather than try to explain the distance from us to the sun by any numerical figure. All the sensations that are caused in our body are brought home to us by the circulating power of our innumerable nerve-veins. These veins spreading all over our body, meet together in our head. Linked like telegraphic wires, they bring messages to the head so that we come to know exactly where we are bitten by an ant, whether the food that our tongues taste is sweet, or a bowl of milk which we hold in our hand is hot. Our body is not as wide as the distance between two telegraph stations, hence we do not take so long to receive a message. Nevertheless, it does take some time, no matter how little. It is so little that it can hardly be measured; and yet the scientists have been able to measure it. They have tested that whatever affects our body reaching our sensitivity runs through our body with a velocity of 100 feet a second. Let us imagine that there is a giant of such a stature who, while his feet are well planted on the earth, his hands reach up to the sun. No matter how powerful the hands of the giant may be, the touch of the sun will burn his hands. But to realize the sensation of the pain an agony of the burn through the nerves will take him nearly 160 years. If he dies before then, he will never be aware of burn.

The diameter of the sun is 864,000 miles. If 110 earths were laid side by side along a straight line, they would be equal to the width of the sun from one end to the other. The sun weighs 330,000 times more than the earth, so that it can exercise its magnetic pull equivalent to that measure. The sun binds the earth to its own orbit by its magnetic pressure, but the earth, due to its own revolutionary speed, is able to keep its distance.

If we pierce a round potato through the middle with a fine rod and let it revolve, its motion will be similar to that of the earth, which to complete one round of its rotation take twenty-four hours. We often say the earth is spinning round on its spinal chord. Where the difference lies between the earth and the pierced potato is that there is no rod through the middle of the earth. In reality it possesses no spinal chord. The imaginary place where the rod could be we refer to as its spinal chord. It is like a top. It spins round one straight, vertical line that is imagined.

To revolve round once on its axis the earth takes twenty-four hours. The sun also rotates on its own axis. How long it takes to complete one round has been found out by a method that must be stated. When in the early morning the sun's glare is not too strong, and you look up into the sun, you perhaps will notice that it has a few black blemishes. Some of these black blemishes appear so magnified at times that they look larger than all the planats and their satellites put together. The smaller marks fade away in no time,but the larger ones remain for two to three weeks longer. When seen through a telescope they seem to be revolving clockwise, but in fact it is the sun that is revolving round carrying all of them. It is by following these black marks that it has been found how long the sun takes to rotate on its axis. It has been proved that the earth takes twenty-four hours and the sun twenty-six days.

These spots in the sun are the huge whirling caves that lie on the surface of the sun's covering. Heated gas keeps emerging from them whirling round and round in serpentine coils from within. The central part of it is deepest black and known as the Umbra. The region surrounding it is not so black, and is called the Penumbra. It appears black because of the surrounding brilliance. If this radiance could be extinguished its luster would be vividly evident. Some of the Umbras in the sun's largest spots measure 25,000 miles from one end to another, and the Penumbras measure 150,000 miles.

Any change in the sun's spots when they increase or decrease has an active influence on the earth in many ways—for instance on the earth's atmospheric air. Almost every eleven years alternately there is an increase and a decrease in these spots.It has been testified that huge tree trunks bear the marks of these years' impact. In a tree-trunk when it is cut, one can see that there are definite ring-marks, each of which represents a year. These marks are sometimes close together, and sometimes they are far apart. From each round mark one can work out how much a tree has grown in a year. In Arizona in America, where the place is almost a desert, Dr. Douglas has made an observation that the ring marks in a tree is much wider in the year when the sun's spots are seen to appear deeper. In tracing out the ring marks for a period of five hundred years in the pines of Arizona it was discovered that during the years 1650 to 1725 there were no such ring marks. Ultimately he found from the recording section at Greenwich, that the sun had hardly any spots during those years.

Out of the prolific ray that comes from the sun's body very little touches the planets. Most of it disappears into the surrounding void, when its speed is 186,000 miles a second. Some of the stars receive its light in four years, some in 30,000 years, and some in 900,000 years. We take it for granted that the sun is our property, and that we have the greatest claim to its gift of light. But it is a very slight portion of the ray that comes and touches us; after that, the messenger light from the sun never returns to it. Where it goes from us, to fulfill what purpose in the universe, nobody knows.

There is a vital thing about the luminary world that has not been discussed yet. How it is incessantly supplied with heat calls for investigation into the atoms. If helium atom can ever be produced in conjunction with an electron and a proton, then in this process of production an energy of an unprecedented nature will be released, the impact of which will bring about an upheaval causing universal destruction. This is where creation is concerned. On the other hand, it needs a much fiercer energy than this to annihilate all matter. If ever there is a clash between a proton and an electron, they will diffuse a stupendous ray before they totally disappear. The energy that will be produced out of this ray is inconceivable.

Such a happening is taking place in the worlds of stars. It is reasonable to surmise that a process of annihilation is active amongst the stars. According to this theory the sun is expending 360,000,000,000,000 tons of material substance every day. But the sun possesses so vast a storage that it can keep up its extravagant expending for many millions of years still. And yet according to the latest calculations the age of the earth has been determined as such that if we accept it, the creation of matter seems a better theory than the theory that matter is being annihilated. If we take it for granted that at some time the sun was a cloud of hydrogen gas, then the energy that ought to be created in the process of hydrogen being developed into helium coincides actually with our present calculation.

Therefore, the scientists have not yet been unanimous on the question whether this universe is heading towards destruction, or is still being created, or is it that both are simultaneously in progress. A few years ago a radiating force was discovered which was named the Cosmic ray, the origin of which could be found neither in the earth, nor in the sun, nor even in our world of stars. The conjecture is that it must have issued forth from some distant skies across the worlds of stars, out of the breaking and moulding processes while the universe was in creation.

However, all the hints of so many contradictory messages that are carried into the scientists' laboratory regrading the creation of the universe, may be leading to wards a solution by helping abstruse calculations. Nevertheless, we are not scientists, we do not understand where exactly mathematics begin, where they can ultimately end. Time began without precedent, centering round a fully-created universe, and that time will finally end with the moment the universe disappears is a conception we find hard to grasp. The scientists will say it is not a question of conception, it is a question of calculation. This calculation is based on the existing state of affairs....if we find darkness before and after, there is no much chance for us.

4

It seems to me that, perhaps, creation is not fettered by rules,
That all the hubbub, meeting and mingling are blind
 happenings of fate,
There is a breaking here, and a moulding there,
Things rise and fall,
Nobody has a view of the sorrow that others go through.

It seems, from behind the unbarred space of the skies,
Creation came flooding with an awesome suddenness.
From some unknown summit,
In the moment's fierce current,
The sun, the moon issued forth, the surging crowd in
 millions emerged.

Somewhere the light fell, somewhere there was night
 darkness,
Somewhere there reigned foaming whiteness,
 somewhere the turbid whirlpool.
Mingling with creation and annihilation
They usurped the ten directions
Stirring up the calm infinite void into quickened ripples.

We are more wisps of straw, rushing along with the stream
There is not a place where we can stand for a moment.
We sink, we rise,
We are eternally revolving round and we fall;
At one moment people come near us, the next moment they
are gone.

In the flowing tumult of creation, who can hear
The wailings of others?
The universe has become deaf with its own howl and roar.
The sighs of thousands of millions
Have composed a buzzing noise,
There is no time to glance black, the restless must move on.

Alas! Love, Alas! affection,
Alas! Love, Alas! affection,
Alas! the heart of man,
From what bordering tree in Paradise
Have you dropped here, losing grip;
You, for whom there is always fear;
You who shrink away from mere touch;
How did you come to be in creation's insentient stream?

Do you sit and listen, O God, you eternal poet,
To all the delirium-prattle of the small man-child?
Truth is the silent portrait
Like the sun at dawn;
Lesser that it is the fabrication
That breaks and builds
The sorcery of imagination.

THE PLANETARY WORLD

It has already been mentioned what planets are. The sun is a star, the earth is a planet—a torn-off fragment from the sun, which, having cooled down, has lost its light. The planets possess no light of their own. All of them have their own destined paths that surround the sun at far and near distances, and are elliptical in shape. It takes some planets less than a year to revolve round the sun, and some more than a hundred years. No matter how long a planet takes to complete its round, the rule of revolution is such that its schedule time is unalterable. All the planets belonging to the sun-family, whether they are large or small, far or near, moving round from the west to the east. From this one can gather that the planets have been flung out of the sun, pushed by the sun's own momentum, so that their movement presses towards the same direction. While alighting from a moving train the body feels a pressure making it lean towards the same way as the train moves. If about half a dozen or more people alight from the same train they will all feel the pressure in the same direction. Likewise, the planets, while being thrown off from the whirling sun, pressed forward with a similar movement. From the tendency of their movement, it has been detected that they are of the same stamp, they are similarly inclined.

Of all the planets Mercury is the nearest to the sun. The distance between them is 35,000,000 miles. It is nearly one-third of the distance that the earth preserves while rotating round the sun. There are some faded marks on the body of Mercury. From these marks it has been observed that one side of its body is turned towards the sun. It competes one round of its revolution in eighty-eight days. It also takes the same time to revolve round its axis. The earth travels nineteen miles a second to revolve round the sun; Mercury exceeds the earth in speed by travelling at thirty miles a second. Because the circuit is much narrower and its speed is more rapid, the time it takes to complete one round of its revolution is one-quarter of that of the earth. The sun does not lie in the centre of the elliptical path of mercury, it is more inclined to one side, so that while revolving Mercury is sometimes nearer to the sun, and sometimes much farther away.

Being so near to the sun, Mercury gets a great deal of heat. A very subtle instrument for measuring heat has been invented. It is known as the Thermo-couple. With the aid of a telescope in conjunction with the Thermo-couple we can verify a lot about heat. According to this instrument the side of Mercury that faces the sun registers a heat that can melt tin or lead. The molecules in the air become so agitated in this heat that they refuse to be held back within the planet. They fail to adhere to their places and run away into space. The molecules in the atmosphere have an escaping nature. On the earth they move at only two miles a second, therefore the earth can resist them by its magnetic pull. But if by any chance, with increase in temperature, the molecules travel at the rate of seven miles a second, it will be no longer possible for the earth to keep its atmospheric molecules under control.

Scientists, who are the scribes of universe records, have to assess the weights of stars and planets as their primary job. This cannot be done by ordinary means of measuring, such as scales; a subtler means has to be propounded to extract the information. This needs to be explained. If for instance a ball thrown hard hit a traveller, and he fell down about five yards ahead, if there were some method by which we could calculate how much must be the weight of the ball in order to displace the man, we could then, by taking into consideration these five yards, work out by this mathematical process the actual weight of the ball. Such a chance of mathematical calculation became possible when the weight of mercury was found out. This chance was feasible due to a comet. Before we go any farther it is better to know what sort of luminary body a comet is.

The word comet means, in Bengali, a 'signal of smoke'. The name has come into being because of its appearance. A round head, and attached to its back a long luminous tail that trails—this is usually the shape. The tail is of a very rarefied gas. So rarefied is it that at time when the earth has come into contact with it, it has not been felt. Its head is of meteorites. All the experts of our day have come to this conclusion that the comets belong to the same group as the sun's satellites. There may, however, be some which do not belong to the sun-family, which are visitors.

Once a violent upheaval took place in the revolutionary path of a comet. As it was passing by the flank of Mercury, it was pushed and drawn by the magnetic pull and was thrown off its track. A derailed train can be lifted back on its rails, but the timetable is set back. So it happened in this case. By the time the comet recovered its usual track the schedule time was over. How great a magnetic pull from Mercury was needed to displace a comet from its fixed path became a matter for mathematical investigation. But it had been an already known fact that the amount of magnetic pull that one exercises depends upon one's weight. So, accordingly, the weight of Mercury was soon detected. It was found that twenty-three planets like Mercury, if placed in a measuring scale, would be equivalent to the weight of the earth.

Immediately after Mercury comes the rotating path of the planet Venus. It takes 225 days to revolve once round the sun. In other words, its one year is equal to our seven and a half months. The speed at which it revolves round its axis is still being debated. Sometimes in the year this planet appears on the west horizon after sunset, when we call it the evening star. It is again seen at times in the eastern sky before sunrise when it is known to us as the polar star. But it is by no means a star. Because it shines so brightly the public have marked it with distinction. This planet is slightly smaller in size than the earth. Its orbit lies 30,000,000 miles nearer to the sun than the earth's orbit—the distance nevertheless is not small. In spite of the fact that the planet is so fairly placed we are still unable to get information about its inner condition. The reason is not that its surface is covered by the sun's glaring light. Mercury is covered by the sun's rays, but Venus hides under its own thick clouds. Scientists have calculated that the heat in the planet Venus can seldom transform water into any other form, so that we can expect both water and clouds to exist on this planet.

As far as can be judged from the upper layer of the clouds, the belief is that the planet has very few resources of oxygen. What has been found is a clear evidence of carbonate gas. The quantity of this gas lying on the top surface of the clouds is many thousand times more than what exists on the earth's surface. This gas is useful on the earth for the purpose of providing food for trees and plants.

A thick layer of this carbonate gas spreads all over the planet like a covering blanket. This heat inside can hardly emerge through it. So that the upper surface of Venus is as hot as boiling water, or perhaps even hotter.

What is astonishing is the fact that no moist gas can be found on Venus. It makes one wonder what can be the possible origin of these thick clouds in the planet. The answer probably is that the top watery surface of the clouds has been congealed to such a state that it cannot possible give out vapour.

This is a point that is well worth considering. At the very first stage when the earth was being created, and the molten substances becoming cooler and cooler began to solidify, giving rise, in the process, to quantities of moist vapour and carbonates. When the heat was further reduced the moist vapour turned into water, forming a sea on the planet. At that time the gases that were supreme in the air were of the inactive kind like nitrogen. Oxygen is a mixer of the ardent type, its nature is to mingle with other substances and create an admixture. Thus it continues to transform itself into other forms. How is it, therefore, that so much oxygen has come to abide in the atmospheric air of the earth?

The main cause lies in the earth's trees and plants. The vegetable world inhales carbon from the carbonate gas in the air to build up its life-element and releases oxygen. Whereas from out of all animals' breath and the putrefaction of twigs and tendrils, carbonates are again formed to replenish their part of the treasury. Perhaps the big chapter in the earth's life-history began when a very scanty proportion of oxygen first came into being in the primeval vegetation. As plant-life tended to grow the quantity of oxygen also increased from the plants' exhaling breath, and the carbonates became less.

Therefore, it seems that conditions on the planet Venus must be the same as when the earth was in its primary state. Perhaps some day by some chance vegetation will appear in the heart of the planet, and out of the carbonates, oxygen will be continuously released. Then, after a long, long period the regime of animals will gradually start. Conditions on the moon and Mercury are quite the opposite. In them the air suitable for life-survival soon became exhausted because of the weakness of their magnetic force.

In the solar system the earth takes the next place to Venus. We shall discuss the earth after dealing with the other planets.

Next to the earth comes the revolutionary range of the planet Mars. Of all the planets this reddish planet is closest to the earth. In size it is nearly one-ninth that of the earth. It takes 687 days to go round the sun. Its orbit round the sun is almost egg-shaped. That is why in its revolution it is sometimes nearer to and sometimes comparatively farther away from the sun. To revolve round its axis it takes only half an hour longer than the earth takes, hence its days and nights are little longer than our days and nights on the earth. The material substance that exists in the planet is one-tenth of the total solidity of the earth, and hence its pulling force is also proportionately less.

Because of the sun's pull the planet Mars should have taken a particular path, and yet a definite change took place in its course. This condition was carried by the earth's magnetic pull.

It is by assessing how much the earth, according to its weight, has been able to shift the planet Mars from its own position that the earth's weight has been estimated. Following this up, the distance of the sun was also detected. For Mars is being pulling by both the earth and the sun, that it has been possible to find out by calculation what must be the distance of the sun at which it would counteract the force of the earth upsetting the equilibrium of Mars. Mars is not a large planet; its weight is relatively small. Consequently, having less force of gravity of its own, there was a danger of its squandering away its atmospheric air. But as it is a good distance away from the sun, it does not get so much heat that the molecules in its air can disappear by evaporation. The search for oxygen in the atmosphere of Mars has proved a failure. There may be a slight quantity of it. From the reddishness of the planet it can be explained that the stone in it, because of its contact with oxygen, has become rusty. Besides, the moist gas that could be traced on it was 2 percent of the quantity that existed on the earth. From all these signs of deficiencies that are found in Mars it is easy to surmise that the earth, by squandering its own resources, will also gradually arrive at a similar state.

The distance between the sun and Mars is greater than the distance between the sun and earth, so that it is certain that the planet Mars is much colder. During the day at the equinox it may retain some warmth, but otherwise at night it is colder in temperature, even below freezing point. As for the snow-hatted north and south poles, there it is colder still.

The snow-clad areas at the south and north poles of the planet sometimes increase and sometimes diminish in size, and sometimes they disappear altogether. The fact that these snows change in size as they melt has been detected by the eyes of a telescopic instrument. The surface of the planet is arid like a desert in many places. Some parts, however, become green-hued in the summer months. Perhaps as the snows melt during these months vegetation sprouts on the tracts where the water flows.

There have been long disputed views amongst the pundits

over the planet Mars. At one time an Italian scientist detected long narrow lines on the planet, when he specified that there must be inhabitants in the planet who, in order to utilize the melted water of the snow, had dug long canals. On the other hand there were scientists who decided that these were but an illusion of the eye. Lately man applied photographic instruments to observe the luminary worlds. The camera-prints also confirm the existence of these black lines. But it will be a sheer guess if we say that these lines are artificial canals, and the handiwork of an intelligent race. It is, however, not impossible that there may be people on the planet, since it holds both water and air.

There are two satellites which revolve round the planet Mars. One of them takes thirty hours to compete its revolution once, and the other takes seven and a half hours—in other words, it moves round three times during the planet's day and night. They finish their revolutionary rounds more quickly than our moon.

There is a great blank space between the orbits of Mars and Jupiter. At this the scientists' curiosity was aroused when they began to investigate. At first four very small planets were visible. Later it was discovered that the space was thronged with thousands of fragmentary planets. All of them were moving about clustering round the sun. We call them 'grahika', which are known in English as 'asteroids'. The first one that was spotted was named Ceres, whose diameter is 425 miles. There is another asteroid named Eros, which in its revolutionary round comes nearer to the earth than any other planet has ever ventured. They are so small that nothing about their inner condition has been available. Collectively they weigh even less than a quarter of the earth's weight. This is less than the weight of the planet Mars, otherwise they would have affected the schedule course of Mars, causing havoc.

All these asteroids can be considered as fragments of whole planets. But the scientists do not believe they are. It is difficult to say why they have not been able to form into whole planets by amassing together.

In addition to these asteroids there are others which are also in groups and must be mentioned. They are very small, they move about also in clusters, and rotate round the sun on their destined orbits. They are a group of meteorites. They come down in ceaseless showers upon the earth; their ashes get mixed with the earth's dust in a quantity that is not negligible. Without the awning of air above the earth it would be quite impossible to save ourselves from the attacks of these diminutive enemies.

The meteorites fall day and night in a greater or smaller measure. But there are occasions when on certain days in certain months they are profuse. On fixed days like 21st April, 9th, 10th, 11th August, and 12th, 13th, 14th and 27th November the showering of meteorites, like fireworks, is worth seeing. Scientists are studying these in order to find a clue to the answer.

The point is that they have their orbits, but their journey, like that of the planets, is not solitary. They are a kind of heavenly body which, like swarms of locusts, form their own groups. Millions of them crowd together as they proceed the same way. On certain days of the year of the earth happens to come within the vicinity of these crowded groups, and they cannot resist its magnetic pull. They come down in a shower and are reduced to dust as they mingle with the earth's dust. Sometimes they fall in larger fragments when they burst and explode, bringing about havoc in every direction. They are a sad example of a comet, which, when it intrudes upon the forbidden heat of the sun, must encounter disaster. There is also another view that the earth at its young age, when in its heart there was more heat, sent up in its volcanic eruptions its innermost substances which rose high and, resisting the earth's magnetic pull, began to revolve round the sun. The earth in its turn, whenever it has a chance of overtaking them, draws them in again. On certain special days they can be seen like votive coins floating about. On the other hand, we are told that there are other meteorites which, breaking away from the solar boundary, are caught up into the earth's magnetic pull. Perhaps there was somewhere at a certain time total destruction and in its force the microcosmic matter exploded, diffusing everywhere. These groups of meteorites are its indication today.

Next to these minute meteorites appears the orbit of the giant Jupiter.

Before we can expect any assured news of the planet we have before us two things for our observation; its distance from the sun, and its size. The distance from the sun to the earth is a little over 90,000,000 miles, and the distance to Jupiter is 483,000,000 miles. In other words, it is over five times more distant than the earth. The heat that Jupiter gets from the sun is one-twenty-seventh part of that received by the earth.

At one time the scientists thought that Jupiter had not cooled down as much as the earth; that it had within itself enough storage of heat; that the restlessness that is seen in its atmospheric orb was because of the heat at its core. But when it became possible to assess the extent of its internal heat it was found to be extremely cold. Its temperature reached to 280^0 Fahrenheit below freezing point. There can be no possibility of moist vapour in Jupiter in this extreme cold. Traces of two kinds of gases were found in its atmosphere. One is ammonia, the smell of which in the leaves at night is strong enough to sharpen one's senses. The other is a gas of the phosphorous kind that has the reputation of luring travellers from the meadow path. By admitting all plausibilities, it has now been confirmed that Jupiter's body is hard, and its density equal to that of the earth. Its stony womb spreads over 22,000 miles. On it lies an outer crust of snow 16,000 miles deep. Then comes a covering layer of air on this solidified ice with a depth of over 6,000 miles. Even hydrogen gas would liquify under the strong pressure of this highly amassed air, so that what has happened in this planet is that a sea of liquified gas has formed on the hard crust of snow. Moreover the surface layer of its atmospheric orb is covered with drops of liquified ammonia.

The planet Jupiter has a gigantic body; its diameter extends to almost 90,000 miles. In size it is 1,300 times that of the earth.

It takes about twelve years for Jupiter to go round sun. Its orbit is no doubt much longer than that of earth because of the distance, but it also has a much slower pace. The earth travels at nineteen miles per second, whereas Jupiter travels at only eight. But on the other hand, in its own circular motion, or rather when pivoting round on its axis, it is very fast. To whirl round its extensive, gigantic body takes ten hours. Within one day and night of our time it completes twice as many days and nights with some left over.

With nine satellites Jupiter makes up its family circle. There is a conjecture about a tenth, which is not yet a certainty. Like moons they rotate round Jupiter but with a much faster speed than our moon. The first four satellites are as big as the moon. They have their brightest and darkest nights, and they wax and wane.

The two farthest satellites of Jupiter move in the opposite direction from that of the other satellites. From this some have gathered that at one time they must have been two asteroids which later caught in Jupiter's pull.

The fact that light travels 186,000 miles a second was first determined from the lunar eclipse of Jupiter. When, according to calculation, the time for eclipse of the satellites was fixed, it was found that each time they came about later than the stipulated time. The reason is that light takes time to appear within our sight. It takes a definite time to move, otherwise the minute there was an eclipse we would see simultaneously all the happenings. It was by measuring the distance from the earth to this satellite, and observing the period of lapse in the scheduled time of the eclipse that the speed of light was first ascertained.

Jupiter has no light of its own. This can be verified from the eclipses of its nine satellites. Let us see how actually an eclipse takes place. When in revolution a planet moves between the sun and a satellite, casting its shadow over the latter, an eclipse of the satellite takes place, it being deprived of the light of the sun. In these circumstances, if the mediary planet had any light of its own, it would have showered its light on the facing satellite, thus wiping out all chances of an eclipse. The eclipse of our moon also tells the same story. When the earth screens the moon from the sun, the lusterless earth can only cast its shadow over the moon; it cannot bestow light upon it.

Next to Jupiter comes the planet Saturn with its orbit.

The planet lies at a distance of 886,000,000 miles from the sun, and to go round the sun once it takes twenty-nine and a half years. Saturn's speed is even less than that of Jupiter—it moves at six miles a second. With the exception of Jupiter it is the largest of all the other planets in the solar system. Its diameter is nine times as great as that of the earth. Though nine times as large as the earth, it takes less than half the time to pivot round on its axis. Because it whirls so fast, it has become, in the pressure of its speed, rather elliptical in shape. It is so immense in size, yet it weighs only ninety times heavier than the earth. Though prodigious in size, its magnetic pull is not more than that of the earth because it is so light weighted. It is encompassed by a covering cloud, the shape and size of which are seen to vary at times.

Saturn has nine satellites. The largest of them is even larger than the planet Mercury. It is 800,000, miles away from the sun and takes sixteen days to complete one round of its revolution.

From observing the spectrum of the surrounding sphere of Saturn it has been noted that parts that are nearer to the planet have a greater speed than the parts that are father away. If this sphere had been like one unbroken wheel, then according to all rules of revolving wheels the outer sides would have greater speed. But if this orb, on the other hand, is made of fragments, piece by piece, then the group that is nearer to the planet will move the fastest in its magnetic pull. Nine large satellites besides these thousands and thousand of fragmentary ones are revolving round the planet Saturn in their different directions.

It is important to mention how these fragmentary groups came to be created round this planet. Because of the attraction of a planet a satellite can never retain its original round shape, it resembles ultimately the shape of an egg. Eventually the time comes when, unable to endure the pull any longer, it breaks into two pieces. These two pieces break again into other pieces. This process continues until there are possibly thousands and thousands of fragmentary pieces form one satellite. The moon is supposed to the heading for a similar fate. Scientists say that every planet is situated in an orb surrounded by an invisible encircling hedge, which may be called the danger zone. Once a satellite is drawn within this enclosure, its body swells, becoming elongated like the shape of an egg, whereupon the process of breaking-up takes place. Finally, all the broken fragments, forming into groups, begin to rotate round the planet. According to the scientists the first satellite of the planet Jupiter has come very near to this invisible line of the danger zone, on entering which it will in no time burst into innumerable pieces. Like Saturn, Jupiter will then be surrounded by an encircling orb of luminaries. Of the encompassing orb of Saturn just mentioned, the scientists maintain the theory that a long time ago one of its satellites happened to drift into this danger zone during its revolutionary round, with the result that it exploded, breaking into pieces which ever since have revolved round the planet.

Because the moon is a long way outside the danger zone of the earth, it has changed very little in its shape. The moon, drawn by the earth's pull, is gradually coming nearer and nearer to it. Ultimately, when it enters the fatal enclosure of the earth's orb, it will burst, exploding into many pieces which will then surround the earth followed by what happened in the case of the planet Saturn. The earth will be thus in the same fatal predicament as the planet Saturn.

A professor at Cambridge, Mr. A. Jeffers, has quite the opposite theory. He maintains that the distance between the earth and the moon is still growing. Eventually, the lunar month will be equivalent to the solar month when the magnetic pull will begin to work, drawing in the moon.

Saturn is farther away from the sun than Jupiter—so it is

even colder. Its atmospheric air on the outer side is very similar to that of Jupiter, with the exception that there is a greater scarcity of ammonia gas on it; the amount of phosphorous gas is more on Saturn than on Jupiter. Though the planet Saturn is a great deal bigger in size than the earth, its weight, comparatively speaking, is not much heavier than the earth. Like Jupiter its atmosphere should be equally dense, as the air has little chance of falling away from Saturn's magnetic force. Because air predominates on this planet, its weight relatively is smaller than its size. Its central hard core has a diameter of 2,400 miles; over this there is a deep covering layer of snow all round nearly 6,000 miles thick. Then comes, finally, 16,000 miles of air spreading all over it.

Next to Saturn comes the orbit of the newly found planet called Uranus.

It has not been possible to find a great deal of information about this planet. In size it is sixty-four times as big as the earth. From a distance of 1,782,800,000 miles from the sun it travels four miles a second, taking eighty-four years to complete one round of its revolution. Though it is of an immense size, we cannot see it without telescopic aid because of its great distance. The components of the planet are slightly denser than water, so that though several times as large as the earth, it is only fifteen times heavier.

To pivot round its axis it takes ten hours and forty three minutes. It has four satellites which revolve round it ceaselessly, pursuing their own individual paths.

Soon after the discovery of Uranus the pundits, observing irregularities in its movement, came to believe that this upset in the rules of the road must have been due to the pull of an unknown planet. After a long investigation they found this planet, which was named Neptune.

Neptune's distance from the sun is 2,793,500,000 miles, and to revolve round the sun once it takes 164 years.

Its diameter is nearly 33,000 miles, and it is slightly bigger in size than Uranus. Through the telescope it looks like a small green saucer. One satellite, keeping at a distance of 222,000 miles from the planet, completes one revolutionary round in five days and twenty-one hours. From the distance of this satellite and the size of the planet it has been ascertained that its substance-mater is a little heavier than water, and it is almost equal to Uranus in size. The speed at which it rotates on its axis is still uncertain.

Even after ascertaining the route that should have been taken by Uranus after making allowances for Neptune's magnetic pull, it was discovered that Uranus still avoided its scheduled path. From this it was gathered that there must be another luminary body beside Neptune outside the orbit of the planet. A new planet was discovered in 1930. It was named Pluto. This planet is so small and at such a distance that it cannot be seen, being even outside the scope of a powerful telescope. That its existence is certain has been proved by a camera from its photographic print. This is the planet which is farthest from the sun, and it receives so little heat from the sun light that we cannot even imagine its possible condition.

From a distance of 3,960,000,000 miles this planet revolves round the sun completing one round in about 250 years.

The planet Pluto has a temperature of 446^0 Fahrenheit below freezing point. In this cold even the most indefatigable gas, being light, becomes solidified. The carbonate matter, ammonia and nitrogen in the air, being frozen, must surround the planet like a hard globe. There are, on the other hand, some people who think that there are many small planets on the farthest edge of the solar world, and Pluto is one of them. But no sure proof has yet been forthcoming. It is doubtful if we shall have any. A far more powerful telescope that is able to raise this distance curtain has yet to be invented to put all disputes to an end.

5

The day when you were all alone
You could not have, indeed, seen yourself.
There was no waiting with eager expectancy for anyone,
Anywhere.
No tear-smeared, fugitive wind
Rushed forth
Sweeping across from shore to shore.

I came, your sleep was broken,
Light broke forth like flowers of joy
In the remote void.
Showering me with fruit and flowers
You made me blossom forth
Turning me, swinging me in exquisite forms.
Hurling me from star to star
You carried me up in your lap.
Hiding me under cover of death
You received me again and again in new forms.

I came, your breast heaved,
I came, your sorrow came,
I came, there came fire-filled joy for you,
There came the tempestuous spring agitating life and death.

I came, that is why you became,
Seeing me, touching me
You touched your own self.

I have shame in my eyes, I have fear in my breast.
A veil shrouds my face.
There is a hindrance to seeing you,
That is why there are tears in my eyes.

Yet, my Lord
I know that
Your desire to see me is eternally roused—
Or what meaning could there be in the sun and the stars?

THE EARTH

Some few facts about the planets regarding their size and movement have been gathered, but the earth is the only planet which, with its entire process of body-building, is adequately known to us. Since the time it began to solidify, taking shape after leaving its gaseous state, marks of history have laid their imprints all over its body.

Having no covering to its outer surface, that part of the earth soon cooled down and hardened, and the lower strata gradually began to solidify. Like boiling milk that forms a skin when left to cool, the upper surface of the earth similarly formed a crust that became more and more wrinkled as the earth still continued to cool down. The unevenness that the wrinkled skin creates on the surface of milk is no doubt very immaterial to us, but the earth with the unevenness of its wrinkled surface, is not a matter that we can so easily dispense with. Because the lower strata had not hardened enough to bear the weight of this uneven surface the top hard layer, without the support of a reliable base began to shrivel and tumble down, giving rise to an irregularity which appeared as mountains and hills. As an ageing man has ridges on his furrowed forehead, so did they appear like folds of wrinkles on the face of the earth. When we consider the size of the earth, the total enormity of its depth, to say that these ranges of mountains and hills are like wrinkled folds on a man's face is not, relatively speaking, a far-fetched analogy.

On the earth in those ancient days on its shrunken, undulating surface there appeared large cavities as there rose high mountains. The cavities had no water in them at the time, for in the heat of the earth even water was in a state of gas. Gradually the earth became cool, the gas turned into water. The cavities filled with water and became seas.

Though most of the moist gas of the earth turned liquid, the main gaseous substances in the air remained gas. It was not easy for them to become liquid. A temperature that could liquify gas would have made the water freeze, so that the world would have been encased in an armour of ice. In a medium mixture of hot and cold temperature all the gaseous matter like nitrogen and oxygen in the air can circulate freely, and we can breathe it to live.

The earth has not altogether stopped shrinking. If in the vibration of this movement the lower stratum somewhere is displaced, the hard outer crust will then crumble, falling with a pressure that will shake the earth's surface, and this will cause an earthquake. Then again there will be places where, under the pressure of the crumbling crust, the hot liquid from underneath will surge up suddenly.

To know the internal conditions of the earth we would have to dig down to a depth that is far out of our reach. In search of coal man has penetrated a depth that is hardly more than a mile. The only account that we have derived from this is that the heat increases at a steady rate as we go down. The increase in the heat is not always even, it differs in degree in different places. There was an accepted theory once that the crust of the earth floated on liquified metal, molten by the internal heat of the earth. But the latest opinion is that the earth is solid. We have evidence enough that there is heat within, but most of the heat comes from energy-giving matter that lies in the strata of the earth. The components of its heart are as solid as iron. It may be extremely hot there but not so hot as to make the material elements inside melt. There material elements within are said to be iron. They spread over with a depth of 2,000 miles. Then comes a covering sheath with the thickness of more than 2,000 miles.

If the earth had been all water, it would have weighed five and a half times less than it weighs mixed as it is between land and water. The stone in its upper crust has density that is three times more than that of water. We have, therefore, to accept the fact that there is heavier matter inside. It is surely not the pressure from the top that has increased its density, the amassed matter inside must be naturally of a heavier weight.

The air that surrounds the earth contains seventy percent nitrogen, and twenty-one per cent oxygen. The remaining gases in it amount to very little. Oxygen is a mixer type of gas. When it contacts iron it makes it rust, when it mixes with carbonate it kindles fire—thus from the atmospheric air a great deal of oxygen is constantly being expended. On the other hand, the trees and plants realize as much carbonate as they need from the carbon-dioxide in the air, and exhale oxygen, replacing it in the air. If it were not so, the earth's atmospheric air would be filled with carbonate only, and man would not be blessed with the air that he breathes.

The air, up to a considerable height in the sky, undergoes very little change. Most of the gases that constitute air are unable to reach up beyond that height. Most probably the atmosphere beyond is a mixture of the two lightest gases, namely, helium and hydrogen.

The air, with the decrease in its density, has risen gradually higher and higher. The meteorites that we see fall on the earth flare up when they come in contact with earth's atmospheric air. As they flare up most of them are seen at first at a height of 120 miles. It must be accepted that there is still more air beyond, and that journeying through it they reach a condition when they blaze.

The light of the sun reaches the earth from beyond a distance of 90,000,000 miles. In crossing this void encircled by planets, it does not seem that light can lose much of its heat. At the first impact of the fierce heat with which the light approaches the contiguous region of its atmospheric orb, the molecules in that area must certainly be reduced to ashes—none can remain intact. The first stratum of these disintegrated molecules thus formed at the highest level of the atmospheric orb is called F_2 stratum.

After expending itself, the surviving sunlight attacks a much denser atmospheric sphere underneath where a new stratum of broken molecules is again established which is named F_1 stratum.

There is yet another stratum of crippled molecules that appears as the sunlight breaks through much denser air at a still lower level, and this has been named E stratum.

The most active ray in the sunlight for destroying these molecules is the violet ray. While bringing about havoc in the upper stratum, the violet ray is impoverished to a great degree before it breaks through the next lower level of the atmospheric orb. And this has been to our advantage. We could never have endured a stronger light.

In addition to sunlight many other destructive forces with their invisible clubs appear from space to deal the air a harsh blow. Like the meteorites that have been mentioned before, they come darting through the planetary sky at a rate of anything between 10 and 100 miles a second. Because of friction with the air, heat is generated in them varying between 3,000^0 to 7,000^0 Fahrenheit. Affected by this, the piercing shafts of the violet ray are unsheathed, and striking against the molecules in the air, reduce them to ashes. Besides these meteorites there is the attack of another ray which has already been mentioned before. It is the cosmic ray. It is the vehicle of the most formidable power in the whole universe.

There are multitudes of minute particles in the oxygen, nitrogen and other gases of the earth's air. They move round incessantly at great speed, and there is constant collision amongst them. The lighter the molecule the faster it moves. The speed of a separated individual molecule exceeds that of a whole group. That is why a single, loose hydrogen molecule is always escaping beyond the range of the earth's outer space, resisting all its pull. And yet, an oxygen or a nitrogen molecule, once outside its group, can never gain the speed of an unrestrained fugitive. For this reason the earth's air has in no way been impoverished, except that the hydrogen which was the earth's chief possession in its young age, has been mostly squandered.

Large-winged birds with wings spread, are often seen soaring in the air for a long while, which makes us realize that the air's density must be sufficient to allow the birds due support.The atmospheric air itself has its own weight besides containing hard and liquid material substances. The air spreads over many a mile between the earth and the sky. The pressure of the air on an article measuring one square foot is nearly 2,214 pounds. The body of an average man receives a pressure that is over 32,800 pounds, and yet it is hardly noticeable. The pressure, as it comes from above, also comes from below, and moreover, the air within our body presses on us and pushes us with an equal velocity, so that we do not find the weight of the air oppressive.

The atmospheric orb like a covering shroud keeps off most of the sun's heat from the earth during the day, and at night it also resists the bitter cold of the greater outer space. Air's covering garment does not rest on the body of the moon so that the moon becomes as hot as boiling water with the sun's heat. Yet, on the other hand, it cools in no time when the earth casts its shadow on it during the time of an eclipse. It could have been saved from the heat if it had air. This is not the only omission we find in the moon. Because it is wanting in air, it is altogether silent; there is no sound anywhere in the moon. When particularly stirred the air raises certain waves of varying lengths, which in turn, with their vibration, strike against the fine skin inside our ears. These waves give rise to different sounds making us automatically respond. When sunlight becomes obstructed for some reason, we find the shade still contains light. It is the air that helps to diffuse light. Otherwise we would only have light where there is direct sunshine. We would have no shade of any kind. Intense darkness would be dwelling side by side by side with fierce light. The blazing rays of the sun would be on the tree-top while underneath there would be jet blackness. While the roof of the house would scorch in the midday blaze, the rooms inside would be as black as the darkest night. The thought of lighting a lamp would have no meaning, as all things on the earth burn because of the oxygen in its air.

The green leaves of the tree contains a round-shaped molecular substance which is filled with a matter called chlorophyll—it is due to this that sunlight is retained in different particles of the tree. The energy that it has produces wood and fruit which are our timber and food in the tree-trunk and its branches. There is very little carbon-dioxide gas in the atmospheric air of the earth. The carbonate components that are in all vegetable matter and from which we get charcoal have their source in this gas. Carbon-dioxide is of no use to man; moreover it is harmful if it is retained in the body. But a tree with the help of its chlorophyll mixes carbon-dioxide with water, producing food for our consumption—food through which we can utilize the energy-giving heat of the sun for our life-substance. We have no power to apply it directly from the air, but the tree can. We borrow it from the tree. The animals of the world give out carbon-dioxide as they breathe, which is useful for the plants and trees. Burning fire and also rotting vegetables and carcasses will give out this gas which will spread in the air. The amount of coal that is burnt in all the workshops and factories of the world and also for the purpose of cooking is by no means small. Carbon-dioxide issues from all these in millions of tons. Thus, what is necessary for the tree as its nourishment is being supplied from wastage.

The air cannot be called an elementary matter, it is an admixture. There is a meeting of many gases in it, but they do not mix. They are together but they are not one. The air contains four times as much nitrogen as it has oxygen. If there were only nitrogen we would be suffocated to death, and with only oxygen in the air our life materials would smoulder to nothingness. These life materials go through a process of combustion, and as they burn they are hindered as well, so that we are able to survive between these two extremes.

The whole atmospheric orb is moist with water. The amount of water the air contains is more than that in a cloud.

It has been already mentioned about the upper strata in the atmospheric orb with their broken luminary molecules. Apart from these there are two natural strata of the air. The first of these two strata nearest to the earth has its scientific name of the troposphere. In Bengali this may be called the 'depression layer'. This rises to a height of 5 to 10 miles from the earth's surface. Compared with the whole range of the atmospheric air the height of the troposphere is very small, and yet in its narrow boundary it contains 90 per cent of the matter that constitutes all. So that the density at this level is far greater than is found on other levels. Because it touches the earth's body,it also contacts the earth's heat. The air here is continually rushing to and fro according to the increase or decrease of this heat. That is why we have rains and storms at this level.The earth's heat cannot reach up to the higher stratum to bring about storms and typhoons. Hence the atmosphere there is calm. The pundits have named this stratum the stratosphere. In Bengali it is the 'motionless layer'.

As the earth emerged from the primaeval sun, so did the moon emerge from the first gaseous-bodied primordial earth. Since then, over millions and millions of years, the earth has been cooling down and hardening: it was the same with the moon.

From the distance of 235,000 miles the moon takes twenty-seven and a quarter days to revolve round the earth once. As it revolves it exposes only one of its sides towards the earth. Its diameter is nearly 2,160 miles, and the substance it is made of is three and a half times heavier than water. Because its distance from the earth is comparatively much shorter than that of any of the other planets, it appears so bright and looks so large in size. Eighty moons would equal the earth in weight. We can clearly see through a telescope that the moon is, like the earth, made of hard substance. There are enormous deep cavities and large high mountains on its surface.

The moon is revolving round the earth because of the earth's pull. To revolve round it once the moon takes a little less than a month. On an average its speed does not amount to more than half a miles per second. The earth moves at the rate of nineteen miles a second. To pivot on its axis the moon takes as much as a month. Its days and years equally pass with the same slow pace.

It has been calculated from the moon's weight that any particle in it with a velocity of one and a half miles a second would probably rush out of its orbit, resisting all its pull. Because the moon basked so much in the sun's rays, the air on its scorched back became very hot with the result that the moon was unable to hold back its atmospheric molecules from escaping. They rushed out beyond all control. Where there is no pressure of air, water turns into vapour at once. The air particles in the moon, as they turned into vapour, became so agitated in the heat that they absconded, breaking away from the moon's resisting hold. Without water and air, we are not aware that life can ever exist. We may easily describe the moon as a lumpy desert place.

Nowadays we do not have to convince anybody that the shooting stars we see at night are not really stars. These meteorites, attracted by the earth's pull, descend on the earth in thousands and thousands. Most of them take fire and are burnt to ashes as they come in contact with the earth's air. Some of the larger ones while still in a blazing state do reach the earth, when, exploding like bombs, they bring devastation to whatever they touch.

There is a continual showering of meteorites on the moon also. The moon has no atmospheric air that can resist the meteorites or turn them into ashes. The body of the moon is bombarded unrestricted by meteorites. They come with a speed that is considerable, at thirty miles a second; they strike on the moon with a force that is deadly.

The large cavities in the moon are caused by volcanoes that were once active. All the molten matter and ashes that emerged from them at the time have not changed their appearances throughout the ages because of the lack of water and air in the moon. Its surface being covered with ashes the rays of the sun cannot penetrate the moon through the deep covering crust, and the heat inside also cannot emerge from it.

The side of the moon that faces the sun has a temperature that is equal to that of boiling water, and the side away from it is so cold that it is 250^0 Fahrenheit below freezing point. During an eclipse when the earth casts its shadow on the moon, the temperature comes down to nearly 346^0 Fahrenheit below freezing point during those few minutes.

Because there is no air, and the sun cannot make a way through the covering ashes, the moon has no storage of heat. That is why it loses its heat so rapidly. From all these instances we are more or less convinced that the moon is covered throughout with volcanic ashes.

The moon is the earth's nearest satellite. Its magnetic pull on the earth is evident in the seas during the cycle of their flow-tide and ebb. Moreover, we are told that all our ailments and fevers and also all rheumatic pains are aggravated by its magnetic pull. People suffering from rheumatism are at their worst during the full moon and the darkest night.

There was no sign of life on the earth in the very beginning. For nearly the first 700,000,000 to 800,000,000 years there were only violent upheavals of wasted energy in various forms throughout. Somewhere perhaps a volcano would breathe out boiling gas, some where it would perhaps emit molten metal, and some where hot water would spring up like a fountain.The surface of the earth would face violent repercussions being pushed from underneath, when mountains and hills would rise, and lands would disappear.

Some 1,500,000,000 years elapsed since the earth's beginning before this primordial restless age of the earth stopped from nearly knocking its own head off and settled down to some degree. It was at this time that the most miraculous incident in creation took place. How and from where life came to be, and moreover, how there was the gradual growth of mind, have left no trace behind. Up to this time there was constant re-shuffling, both destruction and construction in the earth's workshop of creation centering round all inanimate objects. The components concerned were soil, water, iron and stone, etc, and alongside there were a few gases like oxygen, hydrogen and nitrogen, etc. Through different chaotic activities all these resources were thrown into a confusion out of which, through adjustment and overhauling, the mountains, the rivers and the oceans were created, and were equally bartered away in the process. Just then amidst the vastness of this inorganic matter, there appeared life, and along with it mind. This had not the slightest likeness to any other matter that was hitherto existent.

As the first beginning of a star is in the nebula, so what came to be first evident in the animal kingdom of the earth is what we may call the heart's nebula. It is a kind of indefinite, flattened-out life-substance like deeply dense phlegm without the distinction of any limbs—it used to float about in the slightly warm sea water in those days. It is called protoplasm. Like the stars that formed their ingredients from fiery vapour, it also took a period of several ages to form into globules here and there, a particular species of which is named amoeba. They are minute in size, and can only be seen through a microscope. They can be found in the depth of slimy water. They have no eyes, no faces, no limbs. They float about in search of food. By spreading out a part of their own microcosmic body they do the work of feet. When they come in contact with food, they draw it in using these temporary feet. A part of their body they use as a stomach. By dividing and sub-dividing their bodies they increase their species. A branch of this amoeba came into being when it was seen to build a covering shelter round its body like a snail. Millions and millions of minute bodies belonging to this group lie at the bottom of the seas. It was the slime of their bodies as it continued to pile up which formed limestone, creating some of the mountains on the earth.

The fundamental element in the creation of the universe is

an atom. By some inexplicable, special manner these atoms, becoming united, formed the finest repository of life. Each of these life-cells is complete and separate, and possesses within itself a miraculous power by which it nourishes itself by collecting food from outside, rejects the unnecessary and multiplies itself by dividing. It is by this multiplying process, through all loss and death, that the current of life flows on.

In the beginning these minute life-cells when they became visible in the conscious world, appeared singly. But as they began to combine and unite more and more, there was an increase in excellence and diversity in the world of life. As the aggregate of many million stars constitute one nebula, so do these life-cells assemble in millions in one single body. This physical world, raising a constant wave of a geneological order, is proceeding onward with ever new forms. Man's mind for a long while has been occupied with the question of the solar system, the planetary world. But far more miraculous than these is the happening of this conscious world. The earth, cooling down its tremendous heat, taking the shape of one of the lesser planets, came to yield to its humbler fate, and yet it has been possible for life, with mind as its companion, to appear in these very conditions. When we consider this fact, we have to admit that this evolution in the world is the supreme realization. Though there is no proof, and it is doubtful that we shall ever have proof, yet we cannot somehow take it for granted that in the whole universe the right conditions for the survival of life and the awakening of consciousness have been created only on this earth, for according to that it will appear that the earth is the only exception to the entire order of the universe.

6

I exist as a drop; you know that, my innermost God.
I am the pivot on the universe-axis.
'I am'... to realize the fact,
A wonderment possesses my mind,
My heart is hushed under the weight of its mystery.
'I am' and 'others are'...
This needless riddle since the beginning
Has found no answer yet.
The seekers of truth retort,
'Thee is nothing but the one in the universe',
Reducing all to one primordial matter,
Ignoring the mysterious facts of existence,
Which none but you alone know
In this teeming universe.
The primordial essence that lies hidden,
I, as a poet,
Shall acknowledge it in all humility,
Filling my heart ever
With the perpetual wonder of it.

TO CONCLUDE

Once, millions of years ago, there appeared on the young earth a tiny particle of a life-cell which the eye could not see, bringing to us the greatest miracle of a message. What history of magnificence it came to tell, hidden in such mystery! Revealing itself through different tests, through the creation of new bodies that bore the testimony of a rare, rich artisanship, it has been alive ever since. What this intelligence is that lies hidden in it, that is capable of amalgamating, readjusting, innovating and manipulating machinery of great complexity and how through all these it has made itself actively creative amassing successive series of knowledge, these are beyond all our comprehension. Extremely delicate and sensitive by nature these life-cells, according to a geneological order, are assembling at their destined places in the live body, in all parts of the limbs. How through sheer inner urge this miraculous division of labour has taken place in the functioning of the body, one never knows. The cell of the stomach has its specific duty, while the cell in the brain has its work of an entirely different nature. And yet, the atoms in the life-cells are fundamentally the same. At whose command was it that this very abstruse work was allotted in parts, and by bringing about a harmony in their diverse activities how was it ever possible to achieve a congruity that goes by the name of health? The life-cell has two main functions to perform—one to get food from outside for its own nourishment so as to live, and the other to procreate its own kind in order to further its race.This effort of a highly complex nature for self-preservation and the continuation of the race was ingrained in it from the beginning—but how?

All that happens in the animate world has as its background the prelude of a vast lifeless world. The mind becomes aware of these happenings, but behind all this knowing there should be the background prelude of a universe-mind. But one cannot see it in connexion with iron, stone or gas, or anywhere within them. Then one day both life and mind appeared on the earth, bringing an impregnable question with them—in the vehicle of a minute life-cell.

Their advent, in the history of the earth's creation, was unexpected. And yet somehow our intelligence refuses to accept that there are occurrences of an incidental nature which can appear suddenly without any cognition with other things. We can imagine that if there is any root similarity between the inanimate world and the conscious world, it must be the all-pervading energy, or the heat in matter. After a considerable time science has discovered that when we look at matter, however, inert it may seem superficially and devoid of sparks, there is a kind of illuminating process that goes on unobtrusively within it. This illuminating spark in its subtle form manifests itself in life; moreover, it manifests itself further in yet a subtler form in consciousness and mind. As we find there is nothing but this great luminous spark in the beginning of creation, we have to own that this consciousness is its manifestation. By raising layers of coverings one by one from the inanimate to the animate, it is constantly aiming to unfold this greater consciousness in man by gradually removing all its shrouded veils. This evolved freedom of consciousness is perhaps the ultimate destiny of creation.

The pundits say the life-span of this vast universe is gradually decreasing, which has to be faced. Like man's body, the universe is made of heat in the body. The tendency of heat is such that as it expends itself it gradually loses its warmth. The heat on the top surface of the sun has a temperature of 6,000^0 Centigrade. It is with a small fraction of this heat that the air blows on the earth, the water flows, and the animals and beasts with the urge for life are moving around. But their resources are all diminishing. One day, when the extinguishing heat throws up all its energy into the empty void, who is to draw it in making it worthy of a form? A time comes when the ever-active, energy-giving heat in our body becomes a part of the surrounding elements and nothing can bring it back to existence. Whatever is happening in the universe—from the crawling of an ant to the whirling speed of the stars—each is setting in order its town account of expenditure in the records of the universe. However far away it may be, the day will surely come when the universe, through its daily incurred expenses, will finally exhaust its resources of heat, scattering it all into nothingness. According to this, the mathematicians have been busy trying to calculate the date of expiry of the universe.

So have the pundits also fixed the date when the sun, the stars and the other luminaries first came into being, and there is a question in my mind. Where in infinity is the beginning? All arguments about the unreliability of the very beginning and the ultimate ending in infinity can only be dismissed if we can accept what is said in our Shastras, and that is, all creation and annihilation take their turn alternately, each lasting over a period of a Kalpa, a period of 432,000,000 years of mortals, like waking up and going to sleep.

All throughout the solar system, through the diverse movements of the luminaries and their dwellings there runs a supreme masterly order. Different planets keeping the same evenness of distance from their individual orbits, caught in a magnetic whirlpool are pacing in the same direction, each paying in its turn revolutionary homage to the sun. Thinkers who have concerned themselves with the origin of creation have refused to accept that such order in the planets received prominent recognition. What was the greatest hindrance in the way of accepting most of the viewpoints was the disparity in calculation about the revolving speed of the clustering bodies that make up the solar system. When this difference compared with the stipulated speed became farfetched exceeding all limits, the viewpoints were no longer valid. There were a couple of theories which conformed nearly to the schedule speed and have held their ground all this while, but they seem now to be confronted with new obstacles. Recently the director of the Award

Committee at Princeton University of America, Mr. Henry Norris Russell, had expounded a theory contradicting Jeans and Littleton. From him it appears that perhaps both of them will have to retire from the category of the accepted list, and will have their views nullified as in the case of others previously. If at the collision of the stars the planets were created, then the argument is that the long, elongated tail of burning gas emerging out of the collision would have a temperature so high that the whole gaseous mass would be shattered in fragments, scattering all over. On the other hand, having once emitted its heat in rapid succession the elongated thread of gas would cool down, wanting stability of place. In these two activities of opposing forces, in the pull of freedom and bondage, which was the ultimate winner?... This was the theme for discussion in Henry Russell's theory. What is proved to us according to the intricate law of mathematical science is that the molecules in the long gaseous tail being overpowered by the intense heat, became detached and disappeared into the great emptiness. It would have been impossible for them to get back into any form of solid coherence, thus creating the world of planets. The obstacles that Russell has raised in his discussion strike hard at the root of both Jeans's and Littleton's theories, and are about to bring them to dust.

Are you a mere portrait, a painting on a canvas?
Those distant nebulae
That cluster round in the nest of heavens;
Those passengers in darkness
Who with lamps in hand are journeying through day and
night—

The planets, stars and the sun;
Are you not as real as they are?
Or alas! Are you an image, no more than a mere portrait?

In the midst of all that is ever-moving,
Why do you remain still?
Why are you always with the wayfarer?
You pathless One!
Why day and night,
Remaining in the midst of all you are yet afar,
In an eternal seclusion of motionlessness?

This dust,
Raising its grey mantle,
Spreads out on all sides,
Leaning on the wind;
In April changes the widowed appearance
Of the ascetic earth,
Adorns her in ochre-red;

Anoints her body with fragrant substance
For the spring-dawn of union—
This dust is also real,
These grasses,
That are trodden at the feet of the universe
Are variable.
In their variability they are real.
You do not vary, you are an image,
You are merely a painted portrait.

Once you came on the path walking by our side,
There was heaving in your breast,
There was life in your limbs
Creating forms with rhythm ever-new,
In songs and dances,
Beating time with the universal rhythm,
In my life, in my world,
You were so real,
In my eyes it was you
Who painted the world with images
Born of beauty and essence
Under the wielding of your brushes,
You existed in that dawn
As the speech-embodiment of the universe.

In our journey together,
The night came,
And under its screen
You stopped still.
Since then
I have moved on, day and night,
In all my joys and sorrows.
There is that constant ebb and flow
In light and darkness
In the wide expanse of the heavens;
Flowers proceed in silent greetings
Flanking either side of the road;
The unruly life-spring rushes forth

In those thousand-fold torrents
Raising death-knells in her anklets;
An unknown tune
Has thus led me farther and farther away,
I have been intoxicated by the urge of the road,
You stepped out of my road
And where you halted
You remained motionless.
This grass, this dust—those stars, sun and moon,
Behind them all
You remain a portrait, a mere reflection.

What ravings are these of the poet?
Are you indeed an image?
No, no—that cannot be, it is not so.
Who says you are bound
Within the fixture of lines,
In agonised silence?
Surely there is joy
Because the river has not lost yet
The urge of its waves;
Because these clouds
Have not deleted their golden script;
If your reflection
In the long tresses of the forest-trees
Were totally effaced from the earth
Then the shadows of the 'madhavi' creepers
Playful in the vagrant wind with their rustling sound
Would be no more than
A long-forgotten dream!
Or is it that I have forgotten you?

You dwell at the root of my life
That is why perhaps is the mistake.
Absent-minded I walk on—
Do I not ignore the flowers?

Do I not ignore the stars too?
And yet they sweeten the air I breathe,
They fill my forgotten lapses with tune,
It is not forgetting, it is my forgetfulness.
Sitting in the core of my oblivion
You raise waves in my blood.
My eyes do not see you,
You have taken abode in my eyes.
That is why today
You are the green in greenness,
You are the blue of the blueness,
In you
My whole world has found its heart's concord,
Unknown to me, unknown to any,
My songs strike your tune;
You are the Poet in the heart of the poet,

You are no image, you are no painted portrait.
You were with me in one unknown dawn,
Then I lost you at night.
Since then through darkness,
Without my knowledge,
I find you again and again.

You are not an image, you are no painted portrait.